THE LIFE AND TIMES
OF AKHNATON

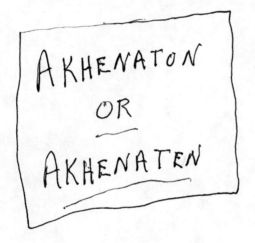

THE LIFE AND TIMES OF AKHNATON

PHARAOH OF EGYPT

ARTHUR WEIGALL
LATE INSPECTOR GENERAL OF ANTIQUITIES,
EGYPTIAN GOVERNMENT

"YE ASK WHO ARE THOSE THAT DRAW US TO THE KINGDOM IF THE KINGDOM IS IN HEAVEN? THE FOWLS OF THE AIR, AND ALL THE BEASTS THAT ARE UNDER THE EARTH OR UPON THE EARTH, AND THE FISHES OF THE SEA, THESE ARE THEY WHICH DRAW YOU, AND THE KINGDOM OF HEAVEN IS WITHIN YOU."

—GRENFELL AND HUNT: *OXYRHYNCHUS PAPYRI*, IV. 6

Cooper Square Press

First Cooper Square Press edition 2000

This Cooper Square Press edition of *Akhnaton* is an unabridged republication of the revised edition published in London in 1922.

Published by Cooper Square Press
An Imprint of the Rowman & Littlefield Publishing Group
150 Fifth Avenue, Suite 911
New York, New York 10011

Distributed by National Book Network

Library of Congress Cataloging-in-Publication Data

Weigall, Arthur Edward Pearse Brome, 1880-1934.
    The life and times of Akhnaton, Pharaoh of Egypt / Arthur Weigall.—1st Cooper Square Press ed.
        p. cm.
    Originally published: London : Thorton Butterworth, 1910.
    Includes index.
    ISBN 0-8154-1092-1 (pbk. : alk. paper)
    1. Akhnaton, King of Egypt. 2. Egypt—History—Eighteenth dynasty, ca. 1570-1320 B.C.
3. Egypt—Religion. 4. Pharaohs—Biography. I. Title.
DT87.4 .W4 2000
932'.01'092—dc21   00-034545

⊖™ The paper used in this publication meets the minimum requirements of
American National Standard for Information Sciences—Permanence of
Paper for Printed Library Materials, ANSI/NISO Z39.48–1992.
Manufactured in the United States of America.

CONTENTS

IV.—AKHNATON FORMULATES THE RELIGION OF ATON

V.—THE TENTH TO THE TWELFTH YEARS OF THE REIGN OF AKHNATON

VI.—THE THIRTEENTH TO THE FIFTEENTH YEARS OF THE REIGN OF AKHNATON

VII.—THE LAST TWO YEARS OF THE REIGN OF AKHNATON

VIII.—THE FALL OF THE RELIGION OF AKHNATON

ILLUSTRATIONS IN THE TEXT

PREFACE

" The Life and Times of Akhnaton " was first published in 1910, and went through two or three editions; but at length it passed out of print, and the few copies which remained in the market were sold at five and six times the book's original price. This continued demand has led to the present re-issue, in which the material has been brought up-to-date and considerable additions have been made, though it has been thought best to leave the text on the whole in its original form.

Great excavations are now being conducted by the Egypt Exploration Society upon the site of Akhnaton's sacred city; and so important is this work, and so widely should its aims be known, that on this account also the re-publication of this volume may serve a useful purpose. Those who chance to have their interest aroused by it should communicate with the Secretary of the Society, 13, Tavistock Square, London, W.C. 1, who will be glad to supply information as to these excavations. Funds are urgently needed for the extension of the work; and, as the reader will realise from the following pages, there is probably no period in ancient history which so merits elucidation, and no site which will so well repay excavation.

When this book was first prepared for the press I was alone in my belief that Akhnaton was only thirty years of age at his death, and my contention that the then recently discovered mummy of a young man of that age was this Pharaoh himself was greatly ridiculed. Time, however, has shown the correctness of my assertion, and the identification, as well as the course and duration of the king's life as given in the present volume, are now generally admitted, except by the well-known German scholar, Professor Kurt Sethe of Göttingen, who, at the time of writing (1922) still finds himself in doubt.

Although the lay reader will not, perhaps, be interested, I think it will be as well to state here in brief outline my general argument for the identification of the mummy and the age of Akhnaton at his death; and I may be permitted to preface my statement by a few words in regard to the excavations which led, in 1907, to the discovery.

The Tomb of Queen Tiy, in which lay the mummy believed to be that of Akhnaton, was discovered in January, 1907, during the excavations which were being conducted by Mr. Theodore M. Davis in the Valley of the Tombs of the Kings at Thebes. Mr. Davis was a very charming American gentleman, who, in his old age, used to spend his winters on a dahabiyeh

at Luxor, and there became interested in
Egyptology. In 1902 he gave a small sum of
money to Mr. Howard Carter, then Inspector-
General of the Antiquities of Upper Egypt, in
order to enable him to conduct some excavations
in the royal necropolis, and in 1903 the Tomb
of Thutmose IV was discovered during the work
carried out with this money. In the same year
the Tomb of Queen Hatshepsut was cleared out
by Mr. Carter, again at Mr. Davis's expense ;
and thus the latter became established, so to
speak, as the banker behind the Egyptian
Government's excavations in the Famous Valley.

In 1904 Mr. Quibell took Mr. Carter's place
at Luxor, and continued these excavations ;
and in 1905 I was appointed Inspector-General,
Mr. Quibell and I jointly working the famous
Tomb of Yuaa and Tuau early in that year.
At that time Mr. Davis was paying for the
actual excavations, but we, the Egyptian Government Department of Antiquities, bore all the
other expenses, such as those of packing the
antiquities, safeguarding the finds, and so forth.
It is interesting to note that the total cost to
Mr. Davis of the season's work which thus produced one of the greatest finds ever made in
Egypt was about £80.

In 1906 I insisted that Mr. Davis should em-
ploy a proper archæologist to conduct the work

under my supervision, and Mr. Edward R. Ayrton was nominated. From that time onwards for the next few years these excavations were carried on in the following manner :— Mr. Davis paid for the actual excavations and was regarded as their nominal director ; an archæologist, paid by him, lived on the spot, and conducted the work ; I supervised it on behalf of the Government and officially took charge whenever any discovery was made ; the antiquities found all went to the Cairo Museum, with the exception of a few objects given as souvenirs to Mr. Davis and now in the Metropolitan Museum of New York, U.S.A. ; the Government bore all working costs other than those of the excavations themselves ; Mr. Davis paid for the publication of the annual volume ; and we all united to give him the credit of the discoveries, the work being deemed worthy of every encouragement, in spite of the fact that its promoter was himself an amateur, and that the greatest tact had to be used in order to impose proper supervision on his work.

The work was being conducted in this manner when the Tomb of Queen Tiy was found. Mr. Ayrton was in charge, and officially handed over to me as soon as the discovery was made ; but, for diplomatic reasons, I kept in the background, and to a great extent left the clearing

of the tomb in his efficient hands, only keeping
an eye on the work. When Mr. Davis published the results, he incorporated a short note
by Mr. Ayrton, but preserved a strict silence
in regard to my own part in the work; and
I should like to explain that this was not in any
way an ungenerous or unfriendly act, but was
due to his very understandable objection to
the restrictions which my Department rightly
obliged me to impose upon him.

Mr. Davis and Mr. Ayrton are now dead, and
Mr. Harold Jones, who helped in the work, has
also passed away. I am, therefore, the only
surviving member of this little company of
excavators, and the above explanation is necessary in order to make clear my own standing
in regard to these excavations, and to give
authority to the statements which I shall make.

In this preface I want to show that there can
be no doubt that the mummy found in the
Tomb of Queen Tiy was that of Akhnaton; and
it will therefore be best to begin by deciding,
from the monuments and other historical evidence, the age at which this king died. The
following arguments may be adduced:—

1. Akhnaton was married to Nefertiti either
before or soon after his accession to the throne.
On the boundary stelae at El Amarna, dated
in the sixth year of his reign he was already

B

the father of two daughters by her. What, then, is the likely age at which he would have become a father ? The mummy of Thutmose IV, his grandfather, has been shown by Professor Elliot Smith to be that of a man of not more than twenty-six years of age. That king was succeeded by his son, Amenophis III, who is known to have been married to Queen Tiy before the second year of his reign. Thus both Thutmose IV and Amenophis III must have been married by twelve or thirteen years of age. Amenophis III was, according to the examination of his mummy by Elliot Smith, about forty-five or fifty at his death ; and, as he reigned thirty-six years, he could have been at most fourteen at his marriage. Akhnaton's daughter, Merytaton, born in the third or fourth year of his reign was married to Smenkhkara before the seventeenth year of the reign, *i.e.*, at thirteen or fourteen. The Princess Ankhsenpaaton, born about the eighth year of the reign was married at latest two years after Akhnaton's death, *i.e.*, when she was eleven ; and the younger princess, Neferneferuaton, was married to the King of Babylon's son when she was probably not more than five or six.

Child-marriages such as these are common in Egypt even at the present day ; and if Akhnaton was, in this regard, like his father and grandfather it may be assumed that he was certainly not older than fourteen when his first child was born. This would make him somewhere round about thirty at his death.

2. In the biography of Bakenkhonsu, High Priest of Amen under Rameses II, we are told that he came of age at sixteen. Now Akhnaton was under the regency of his mother during the first years of his reign, as the Tell El Amarna letters and the Wady Hammamât inscription prove ; and one may thus assume that he was then under age. If, as seems probable, the great changes in art and religion began when he came of age, say in the third or fourth year of his reign (and the King speaks of the fourth year in this connection in the foundation inscription), he would be just about thirty at his death. In this regard it is worthy of note that the Caliph El Hakkîm was sixteen when he issued his first religious decrees.

3. When Yuaa and Tuau were buried, probably quite late in the reign of Amenophis III, since both were of an advanced age according to Professor Elliot Smith, that King, and Queen Tiy, and two of their daughters gave presents of funeral furniture, but there is no mention yet of a son. Nor have we any evidence of Akhnaton's existence until late in the reign when his marriage to Tadukhipa of Mitanni

was arranged. On the Medinet Habu colossus three of Tiy's daughters are shown, but there is no reference yet to a son. We should surely have some mention of him had he been living during the main years of his father's reign; and the inference thus is that he was still very young at his father's death.

4. Amenophis III seems to have been in ill-health during the last years of his reign, for on two occasions the King of Mitanni sent a miracle-working statuette of the goddess Ishtar to him in the hope that it might cure him. And there is the curious fact that Manetho gives only thirty years for his reign, whereas there is contemporary evidence that he reigned for thirty-six, the explanation being, probably, that he was unfit to govern during the last six years of his reign. Yet his son did not assume office, and the power evidently remained in the hands of Queen Tiy. Akhnaton, therefore, must have still been very young; and even when he came to the throne the Tell El Amarna letters show that his mother had still to be consulted in affairs of state. On the other hand a letter from Dushratta, docketed in the thirty-sixth year of the reign of Amenophis III, refers to Tadu-khipa as being already married to Akhnaton, which indicates that the boy was twelve or thirteen by then. This would make his age

at his death, seventeen years later, just about thirty.

In view of the above arguments I do not see that it is possible to suppose that Akhnaton was more than thirty years of age at his death. On the other hand, there is at Oxford a fragment which shows the King celebrating his *heb-sed*, or Jubilee, and which, therefore, at first sight indicates that he was much older. I do not think, however, that anything definite can be deduced from the occurrence of this festival. The *heb-sed* festival was generally thought to have been held after a king had reigned thirty years; but Professor Sethe has shown that it was more probably a festival held thirty years after a king had become heir to the throne. Now Akhnaton was heir immediately on his birth, and, if Sethe is right, the celebration of the jubilee would thus only indicate that he was at least thirty years of age at his death, a fact which is in accord with the above arguments. There is nothing on the Oxford fragment[1] to indicate the date at which this jubilee occurred, but the fact that a " High Priest of Akhnaton " is mentioned thereon suggests that it belongs to the last years of the reign, since this looks like a late and advanced development of the Aton religion. Edward

1 Prof. Sethe is wrong in thinking that the cartouches on this fragment show signs of the earlier spelling.

Meyer, however, has pointed out that Thutmose
II, whose mummy shows him to have died before
he was thirty, seems to have celebrated his
jubilee twice. Akhnaton may thus have held
this festival at an equally early date.

The mummy which we found in the tomb
of Queen Tiy, and which rested in a coffin un-
doubtedly belonging to Akhnaton, was sent by
me to Professor Elliot Smith in Cairo for examination. I may mention, in order to debar any
possible suggestion of confusion or mistake in
regard to the body, that I soaked the bones
in paraffin wax so as to preserve them, and that
the bones examined by Elliot Smith were thus
distinguished. His report on them was published in his catalogue of the royal mummies
in the Cairo Museum.

In regard to the age, after an exhaustive
examination of the condition of the skeleton,
he comes to the conclusion that although many
of the data suggest an age of about twenty-six
years, "no anatomist would be justified in
refusing to admit that this individual may have
been several years younger or older than this
estimate"; and he goes on to say that if the
historian can produce proofs to show that
Akhnaton was as old as thirty at his death,
the anatomical evidence which suggests an
earlier age would have to be considered too

slight to weigh against that conclusion. Thus,
so far as the age of the body is concerned, the
mummy may be regarded as fulfilling the conditions necessary for its identification with
Akhnaton.

As to the physical features, the following
facts from the report are important. (1) The
configuration of the upper part of the face,
including the forehead, is identical with that
of Akhnaton's maternal grandfather, Yuaa.
(2) The jaw is typically Armenoid, as might
be expected in view of the fact that Akhnaton's
paternal grandmother was Mutemua, a princess
of Mitanni. (3) The projection of the upper
incisors is similar to that found in many members of the royal family of the Eighteenth
Dynasty. (4) A curious and unusual bony
ridge passing from the nasal spine to the alveolar
point in this skull occurs also as a peculiarity
of the skull of Amenophis III. (5) There are
points of resemblance to Amenophis III, also,
in the molar teeth. (6) The general structure
of the face, and especially the jaw, is exactly
that portrayed in the statues of Akhnaton.

These physical features prove pretty con-
clusively that the mummy is that of a male
member of the royal family, who had in his
veins the blood both of Yuaa and Amenophis
III, and the objects found with it prove that

it is to be dated to the period of Akhnaton.
Thus the body, so far as the known historical
facts go, could only be that of Akhnaton. There
is nobody else whom it could be, and this is
a negative argument which must be given prominence throughout.

As to the evidence of the coffin and other
objects found with the body. The coffin, now
exhibited in the Cairo Museum, is that of Akhnaton without any question, for it is inscribed
with his name and titles, on the top of the lid,
inside the lid, and inside the shell. But there
is one fact which, by some most mysterious
circumstance, has been obscured. A great deal
of rain-water had dripped into the tomb through
a fissure in the rock, and the mummy—flesh
and bandages—had rotted away. But when we
removed the lid of the coffin, we found a band
or ribbon of thin gold foil which had evidently
passed down the front of the mummy, outside
the wrappings, and, at right angles to this, other
bands which had passed round the body. When
we had gathered up the bones and fragments
and dust we found another similar band which
had evidently passed down the back of the
mummy. These bands were about two inches
wide and were inscribed with the titles of Akhnaton, but the cartouche was in each case cut
out, so that there was simply an oval hole in

the band wherever it occurred. The cartouches
of Akhnaton, it is to be noted in this connection,
were likewise erased in the coffin-inscription.

I must now give a brief description of the
tomb and such of its contents as are pertinent,
which should be read in connection with Mr.
Davis's and Mr. Ayrton's account of the discovery published in the former's big volume.

The tomb was a rock-cut chamber approached
by a sloping passage. It was similar to the
tomb of Yuaa and Tuau, and was thus the sort
of sepulchre one might expect to be made for
a queen or other royal personage who was not
actually a reigning sovereign. In it were the
remains of a large box-like wooden shrine or
canopy which had evidently contained a coffin
and mummy. The inscriptions leave no doubt
that this was made for Queen Tiy's burial by
Akhnaton, and four foundation bricks are also
inscribed with Akhnaton's name. A number
of small objects inscribed with the Queen's name
also belonged to this the original burial in the
tomb. The sides of the shrine or canopy had
been taken to pieces, and one side lay in the
passage, as though an attempt had been made
to remove it at the same time that the mummy
of the queen was removed, but that the work
had been abandoned owing to the narrowness
of the passage.

Thus there can be no reasonable doubt that the tomb was made for Queen Tiy, and that her body was removed at a later date, the large shrine or canopy being left behind because of the difficulty of taking it out, and some of the small objects being overlooked.

But in another part of the chamber we found the coffin of Akhnaton. Originally it had lain upon a bier, but this had rotted away and collapsed, and in the fall the mummy had been jerked partly out of the coffin, so that the head of the body projected somewhat from under the lid. Photographs of it as we found it are published in Mr. Davis's volume. Near the coffin were four canopic vases which will be discussed later.

Scattered about in the rubbish were fragments of small clay sealings inscribed with the name of King Tutankhamen. The entrance of the tomb showed the remains of at least two closings up. There was part of an original wall of rough limestone blocks cemented on the outside, and above the ruins of this there was a second and more loosely constructed wall. On fragments of the cement were impressions of a seal representing a jackal crouching over nine captives—the usual seal of the necropolis. The second wall had been partly pulled down and had not been built up again.

I interpret the above facts in the following manner :—Firstly, Queen Tiy was buried in this tomb, but it was entered later by the agents of Akhnaton whose orders were to erase the name of Amen wheresoever it was to be found. After Akhnaton had died and had been buried at El Amarna, the court returned to Thebes under King Tutankhamen. The body of Akhnaton was then brought to the old necropolis of his fathers and was placed in this tomb of his mother. A few years later when his memory came to be hated, the priests removed the mummy of Tiy from the tomb which had been polluted by the presence of " that criminal," as Akhnaton was now called, erased the king's name, and left him the solitary and nameless occupant of the sepulchre.

Mention has been made of the four canopic jars. These obviously do not belong to Queen Tiy ; for the men who removed the queen's mummy from the tomb would not have left her heart, viscera, etc. behind. By the same token the jars belong to the mummy which we found in the tomb. The contents of the jars have rotted away, as had the flesh on the mummy, owing to the damp. Only such fragments of their wrappings as were well covered with bitumen are now to be found in the jars. (See Daressy on p. 24 of Mr. Davis's volume).

On each jar there has been an inscription, presumably giving the owner's name ; but in each case this has been entirely erased. The lids of the jars are each carved in the form of a royal head, wearing an ordinary wig which might be either that of a male or female, but having a king's single uræus on the forehead. The queens of this period have a double uræus, as may be seen, for instance, on the Sinai head of Tiy, on the Userhat relief of that queen at Brussels, on her Medinet Habu colossus now at Cairo, on the Fayûm head of this period now in Berlin, on various reliefs of Nefertiti, notably that shown in Petrie's History, ii, p. 230, and so forth. The fact that these canopic heads have no beard does not suggest that they are female, for I do not think Akhnaton is ever shown with a beard. The heads might well be portraits of Akhnaton executed somewhat early in the reign, and the characteristic lower jaw is quite noticeable in at least one of the four, as Daressy also has pointed out.

I think the reasoning should follow these lines :—The canopics are not those of Tiy, for if they were they would have been removed with her mummy, being an essential part of the mummy ; and moreover there would have been a double uræus on the forehead. But if they do not belong to a queen they must certainly

belong to a king, and what king other than
Akhnaton could they possibly represent?
Canopic jars, however, would never be inten-
tionally separated from the mummy whose
heart, etc. they contained ; and thus, if the
jars are those of Akhnaton then the presumption
is that the mummy must be that of Akhnaton
also.

The fact that these canopic jars seem, by the
style of the portraiture, to date from several
years before Akhnaton's death is interesting,
as suggesting that he had caused his funeral
outfit to be made ready for him in anticipation.
There are two other facts which lead to the
same conclusion. Firstly, in the inlaid inscription which runs down the front of his coffin the
word "truth" is written with the sign of the
goddess, a sign which was not used in the late
years of the reign. On the other hand, the
inscriptions on the foot of the coffin, and on the
inside of the lid and shell, show this word spelt
out in the later manner. Thus, we may suppose
that the coffin was begun, though not finished,
early in the reign. That it was finished later
is also shown by the appearance of the later
form of the cartouche of the god Aton on the
uræus at the forehead of the effigy on the lid.
Secondly, amongst the debris of the mummy
a necklace ornament and a piece of gold foil

were found, each inscribed with the earlier form
of this Aton cartouche. This shows that some
parts, if not all, of the burial equipment were
prepared several years before they were actually
required. Such a procedure, however, is not
surprising. A Pharaoh always caused his tomb
to be prepared during his reign, and it is to be
presumed, therefore, that the coffin and funeral
outfit were also made ready at the same time.
And, indeed, it may be argued that these proofs
of the early date of the coffin and mummy
ornaments explain why the heads of the canopic
jars show a rounder, younger, and less peculiar
face than is seen in the later portraits of Akhnaton ; and thus the identification is strengthened.

Over the face or head of the mummy we
found an object in the form of a vulture, made
of gold, and slightly curved so as to fit over the
bandages. Mr. Davis and M. Daressy call it
a queen's crown, and M. Maspero caused it to
be labelled as such in the Cairo Museum. It
is, however, no crown ; a conclusion which is
apparent from the fact that it was found with
the tail and not the head projecting over the
forehead. It is simply a sort of pectoral of the
usual form seen in the wall-paintings in the
Theban tombs (for example, that of Horemheb,
No. 78) as part of a mummy's equipment.

To sum up :—The mummy lay in the coffin

of Akhnaton, was enclosed in bands inscribed with Akhnaton's name and was accompanied by the canopic jars of Akhnaton. It was that of a man of Akhnaton's age, the facial structure corresponds to the portraits of Akhnaton, and it has physical characteristics similar to those of Akhnaton's father and grandfather. How, then, can one possibly doubt its identity ? Professor Sethe, however, published in the Nachrichten der K. Gesellschaft der Wissenschaften zu Göttingen in 1921 an article in which he comes to the conclusion that the mummy we found was perhaps not that of Akhnaton ; but it is evident that all the facts were not marshalled before him when he set himself to question an identification which surely is not open to doubt.

ARTHUR WEIGALL.

London, June, 1922.

I

THE PARENTS AND GRANDPARENTS
OF AKHNATON

1. INTRODUCTION

THE reign of Akhnaton,[1] for seventeen years
Pharaoh of Egypt (from B.C. 1375 to 1358),
stands out as the most interesting epoch in the
long sequence of Egyptian history. We have
watched the endless line of dim Pharaohs go by,
each lit momentarily by the pale lamp of our
present knowledge, and most of them have left
little impression upon the mind. They are so
misty and far off, they have been dead and gone
for such thousands of years, that they have
almost entirely lost their individuality. We call
out some royal name, and in response a vague
figure passes into view, stiffly moves its arms,
and passes again into the darkness. With one
there comes the muffled noise of battle; with

[1] Some philologists, preferring to give the value "I" to the initial
letter of the name, call the King "Ikhnaton" instead of "Akhnaton."
The reading "Khuenaten," sometimes found in earlier works, is
incorrect.

c

another there is laughter and the sound of music ; with yet another the wailing of the oppressed drifts by. But at the name of Akhnaton there emerges from the darkness a figure more clear than that of any other Pharaoh, and with it there come the singing of birds, the voices of children, and the scent of many flowers. For once we may look right into the mind of a king of Egypt and may see something of its workings ; and all that is there observed is worthy of admiration. Akhnaton has been called " the first individual in human history " ;[1] but if he is thus the first historical figure whose personality is known to us, he is also the first of all human founders of religious doctrines. Akhnaton may be ranked in degree of time, and, in view of the new ground broken by him, perhaps also in degree of genius, as the world's first idealist ; and, since in all ancient Oriental research there never has been, and probably never will be, brought before us a subject of such intellectual interest as this Pharaoh's religious revolution, which marks the first point in the study of advanced human thought, a careful consideration of this short reign deserves to be made.

The following pages do not pretend to do more than acquaint the reader with the subject, as interpreted in the light of recent discoveries.

[1] Breasted : A History of Egypt.

A series of volumes have been issued by the Egypt Exploration Fund,[1] in which accurate copies are to be found of the reliefs, paintings, and inscriptions upon the walls of the tombs of some of Akhnaton's disciples and followers. In the year 1893 Professor Flinders Petrie excavated the site of the city which the Pharaoh founded, and published the results of his work in a volume entitled " Tel el Amarna".[2]

Shortly before the late war the Germans made some valuable excavations in Akhnaton's city, and discovered amongst other things the studio of a sculptor in which several great works of art, now in Berlin, were found ; and soon after the war the Egypt Exploration Society began its work on the site, which, year by year, is revealing the marvels of that amazing epoch in Egyptian history.

In 1906 Professor J. H. Breasted devoted some space to a masterly study of this period in his " History of Egypt " and " Ancient Records of Egypt."[3] From these publications, and from the Journals of the Egypt Exploration Society, the reader will be able to refer himself to the remaining literature dealing with the subject ;

[1] N. de G. Davies : The Rock Tombs of El Amarna. 5 vols. The Egypt Exploration Fund is the earlier name of the Egypt Exploration Society.

[2] Now out of print.

[3] Published by the Chicago University.

but he should bear in mind that the discovery[1] of the bones of Akhnaton himself, which have shown us how old he was when he died—namely, about thirty years of age—have modified many of the deductions in the earlier works. Those who have travelled in Egypt will probably have visited the site of Akhnaton's city, near the modern village of El Amarna ; and in the museums of Cairo, London, Paris, Berlin, Vienna, Leiden, and elsewhere, they will perhaps have seen some of the relics of his age.

During the early years of the present century an extraordinary series of discoveries was made in the Valley of the Tombs of the Kings at Thebes. In 1903 the tomb of Thutmosis IV, the paternal grandfather of Akhnaton, was discovered ; in 1905 the tomb of Yuaa and Tuau, the maternal grandparents of Akhnaton, was found ; in 1907 Akhnaton's body was discovered in the tomb of his mother, Queen Tiy ; and in 1908 the tomb of the Pharaoh Horemheb, one of the immediate successors of Akhnaton, was brought to light. At all but the first of these discoveries the present writer had the good fortune to be in charge ; and a particular interest in the period was thus

---

[1] As will be recorded at the end of this volume, the body of Akhnaton was discovered at Thebes early in 1907 by Mr. Theodore M. Davis, and the party financed by him, under the supervision of the Egyptian Government Department of Antiquities in the person of the present writer.

engendered, of which the following sketch, prepared during an Upper Egyptian summer, is an outcome. It must be understood, however, that a volume written at such times as the exigencies of official work allowed—partly in the shade of the rocks beside the Nile, partly at railway-stations or in the train, partly amidst the ruins of ancient temples, and partly in the darkened rooms of official quarters during the heat of the day—cannot claim the value of a treatise prepared in an English study where books of reference are always at hand. It is believed, however, that no errors have been made in the statement of the facts; and the deductions drawn therefrom are frankly open to the reader's criticism. There will certainly be no two opinions as to the originality, the power, and the idealism of the Pharaoh whose life is now to be outlined.[1]

2. THE ANCESTORS OF AKHNATON

The Eighteenth Dynasty of Egyptian kings took possession of the throne of the Pharaohs in the year 1580 B.C., over thirteen hundred years after the building of the great pyramids, and some two thousand years after the beginning of dynastic history in the Nile Valley. The founder

[1] The writer has to thank the editors of "The Quarterly Review," "Blackwood's Magazine," and "The Century Magazine," for permitting him to embody in this volume certain portions of articles contributed by him to the pages of those journals.

of the dynasty was the Pharaoh Ahmose I. He drove out the Asiatics who had overrun the country during the previous century, and pursued them into the heart of Syria. His successor, Amenophis I, penetrated as far as the territory between the Orontes and the Euphrates; and the next king, Thutmosis I, was able to set his boundary-stone at the northern limits of Syria, and thus could call himself the ruler of the entire east end of the Mediterranean, the emperor of all the countries from Asia Minor to the Sudan. Thutmosis II, the succeeding Pharaoh, was occupied with wars in his southern dominions; but his successor, the famous Queen Hatshepsut, was able to devote the years of her reign to the arts of peace.

She was followed by the great warrior Thutmosis III, who conducted campaign after campaign in Syria, and raised the prestige of Egypt to a point never attained before or after that time. Every year he returned to Thebes, his capital, laden with the spoils of Asia. From the capture of the city of Megiddo alone he carried away 924 splendid chariots, 2,238 horses, 2,400 head of various kinds of cattle, 200 shining suits of armour, including those of two kings, quantities of gold and silver, the royal sceptre, the gorgeous tent of one of the kings, and many minor articles. Booty of like value was brought in from other shattered kingdoms, and the Egyptian treasuries were full to overflowing. The temples of the gods also received their share of the riches, and their altars groaned under the weight of the offerings. Cyprus, Crete, and perhaps the islands of the Ægean, sent their yearly tribute to Thebes, whose streets, for the first time in history, were thronged with foreigners. Here were to be seen the long-robed Asiatics adorned with jewels made by the hands of Tyrian craftsmen ; here were chariots mounted with gold and electrum drawn by prancing Syrian horses ; here were Phœnician merchants with their precious wares stripped from the kingdoms of the sea ; here were negroes bearing their barbaric treasures to the palace. The Egyptian soldiers held their heads high as they walked through these streets, for they were feared by all the world. The talk was everywhere of conquest, and the tales of adventure now related remained current in Egypt for many a century. War-songs were composed, and hymns of battle were inscribed upon the temple walls. The spirit of the age will be seen in the following lines, in which the god Amon addresses Thutmosis III :—

" I have come, giving thee to smite the princes of Zahi,
I have hurled them beneath thy feet among their high-
     lands . . .
Thou hast trampled those who are in the districts of Punt,

> I have made them see thy majesty as a circling star . . .
> Crete and Cyprus are in terror . . .
> Those who are in the midst of the great sea hear thy roarings;
> I have made them see thy majesty as an avenger,
> Rising upon the back of his slain victim . . .
> I have made them see thy majesty as a fierce-eyed lion,
> While thou makest them corpses in their valleys . . ."

It was a fierce and a splendid age—the zenith of Egypt's great history. The next king, Amenophis II, carried on the conquests with a degree of ferocity not previously apparent. He himself was a man of great physical strength, who could draw a bow which none of his soldiers could use. He led his armies into his restless Asiatic dominions, and having captured seven rebellious Syrian kings, he hung them head downwards from the prow of his galley as he approached Thebes, and later sacrificed six of them to Amon with his own hand. The seventh he carried up to a distant city of the Sudan, and there hung him upon the gateway as a warning to all rebels. Dying in the year 1420 B.C., he left the throne to his son, Thutmosis IV, the grandfather of Akhnaton, who at his accession was about eighteen years of age.[1]

3. THE GODS OF EGYPT

With the reign of Thutmosis IV we reach a period of history in which the beginnings are to

[1] Page 95.

be observed of certain religious movements, which become more apparent in the time of his son Amenophis III and his grandson Akhnaton. We must look, therefore, more closely at the events of this reign, and must especially observe their religious aspect. For this reason, and also in order that the reader may the more readily appreciate, by contrast, the pure teachings of the Pharaoh whose life forms the subject of the following pages, it will be necessary to glance at the nature of the religions which now held sway. Egypt had at this time existed as a civilised nation for over two thousand years, during the whole of which period these religious beliefs had been developing ; and now they were so engrained in the hearts of the people that changes, however slight, assumed revolutionary proportions, requiring a master-mind for their initiation, and a hand of iron for their carrying into execution. At the time of which we now write, this mind and this hand had not yet come into existence, and the old gods of Egypt were at the zenith of their power.

Of these gods Amon, the presiding deity of Thebes, was the most powerful. He had been originally the tribal god of the Thebans, but when that city had become the capital of Egypt, he had risen to be the state god of the country. The sun-god Ra, or Ra-Horakhti, originally the

deity of Heliopolis, a city not far from the
modern Cairo, had been the state god in earlier
times, and the priests of Amon contrived to
identify the two deities under the name " Amon-
Ra, King of the Gods." Amon had several
forms. He was usually regarded as a man of
shining countenance, upon whose head two tall
feathers arose from a golden cap. Sometimes,
however, he assumed the form of a heavy-horned
ram. Sometimes, again, he adopted the appearance of a brother god, named Min, who was later
identified with the Greek Pan ; and it may be
mentioned in passing that the goat-form of the
Greek deity may have been derived from, or connected with, this Min-Amon of the Thebans. On
occasions, Amon would take upon himself the likeness of the reigning Pharaoh, choosing a moment
when the monarch was away or was asleep,
and in this manner he would obtain admittance
to the queen's bed-chamber. Amenophis III
himself was said to be the son of a union of this
nature, though at the same time he did not deny
that his earthly father was Thutmosis IV. Amon
delighted in battle, and gave willing assistance
to the Pharaohs as they clubbed the heads of
their enemies or cut their throats. It is possible
that, like other of the Egyptian gods, he was
but a deified chieftain of the prehistoric period
whose love of battle had never been forgotten.

The goddess, Mut, "the Mother," was the consort of Amon, who would sometimes come to earth to nurse the king's son at her breast. By Amon she had a son, Khonsu, who formed the third member of the Theban trinity. He was the god of the Moon, and was very fair to look upon.

Such were the Theban deities, whose influence upon the court was necessarily great. The Heliopolitan worship of the sun had also a very considerable degree of power at the palace. The god Ra was believed to have reigned as Pharaoh upon earth in the dim ages of the past, and it was thought that the successive sovereigns of Egypt were his direct descendants, though this tradition actually did not date from a period earlier than the Fifth Dynasty. "Son of the Sun" was one of the proudest titles of the Pharaohs, and the personal name of each successive monarch was held by him in the official titulary as the representative of Ra. While on earth Ra had had the misfortune to be bitten by a snake, and had been cured by the goddess Isis, who had demanded in return the revealing of the god's magical name. This was at last told her; but for fear that the secret would come to the ears of his subjects, Ra decided to bring about a general massacre of mankind. The slaughter was carried out by the goddess Hathor in her form of Sekhmet, a fierce lion-headed woman, who delighted to wade in streams of blood ; but when only the half of mankind had been slain, Ra repented, and brought the massacre to an end by causing the goddess to become drunk, by means of a gruesome potion of blood and wine. Weary, however, with the cares of state, he decided to retire into the heavens, and there, as the sun, he daily sailed in his boat from horizon to horizon. At dawn he was called Khepera, and had the form of a beetle ; at noon he was Ra ; and at sunset he took the name of Atum, a word probably connected with the Syrian Adon, "Lord," better known to us in its Greek translation " Adonis." As the rising and the setting sun—that is to say, the sun near the horizon—he was called Ra-Horakhti, a name which the reader must bear in mind.

The goddess Isis, mentioned in the above tradition, was the consort of Osiris, originally a Lower Egyptian deity. Like Ra, this god had also reigned upon earth, but had been murdered by his brother Set, his death being ultimately revenged by his son Horus, the hawk. Thus Osiris, Isis, and Horus formed a trinity, which at this time was mainly worshipped at Abydos, a city of Upper Egypt, where it was thought that Osiris had been buried. Having thus ceased to live upon earth, Osiris became the great King of the Underworld, and all persons prayed to him for their future welfare after death.

Meanwhile Horus, the hawk, was the tribal god of more than one city. At Edfu he was worshipped as the conqueror of Set; and in this manifestation he was the husband of Hathor, the lady of Dendereh, a city some considerable distance from Edfu. At Ombos, however, Set was worshipped, and in the local religion there was no trace of aught but the most friendly relations between Set and Horus. The goddess Hathor, at the same time, had become patron of the Western Hills, and in one of her earthly forms—namely, that of a cow—she is often represented emerging from her cavern in the cliffs.

At Memphis the tribal god was the little dwarf Ptah, the European Vulcan, the blacksmith, the artificer, and the potter of the gods. In this city also, as in many other districts of Egypt, there was a sacred bull, here called Apis, who was worshipped with divine honours and was regarded as an aspect of Ptah. At Elephantine a ram-headed deity named Khnum was adored, and there was a sacred ram kept in his temple for ceremonial purposes. As Khnum had some connection with the First Cataract of the Nile, which is situated near Elephantine, he was regarded as of great importance throughout Egypt. Moreover, he was supposed by some to have used the mud at the bottom of the Nile to form the first human being, and thus he found a place in the mythology of several districts.

A vulture, named Nekheb, was the tribal deity of the trading city of Eileithiaspolis; a ferocious crocodile, Sebek, was the god of a second city of the name of Ombos; an ibis, Thoth, was that of Hermopolis; a cat, Bast, that of Bubastis; and so on—almost every city having its tribal god. Besides these there were other more abstract deities: Nut, the heavens, who, in the form of a woman, spread herself across the sky; Seb, the earth; Shu, the vastness of space; and so forth. The old gods of Egypt were indeed a multitude. Here were those who had marched into the country at the head of conquering tribes; here were ancient heroes and chieftains individually deified, or often identified with the god whom their tribe had served; here were the elements personified; here the orbs of heaven which man could see above him. As intercourse between city and city became more general, one set of beliefs had been brought into line with another, and myths had developed to explain the discrepancies.

Thus in the time of Thutmosis IV the heavens were crowded with gods; but the reader will do well to familiarise himself with the figure of Amon-Ra, the god of Thebes, who stood above them all, and with Ra-Horakhti, the god of Heliopolis. In the following pages the lesser denizens of the Egyptian Olympus play no great part, save as a routed army hurled back into the ignorant darkness from which they came.

4. THE DEMIGODS AND SPIRITS—THE PRIESTHOODS

The sacred bulls and rams mentioned above were relics of an ancient animal-worship, the origin of which is lost in the obscurity of pre-history. The Egyptians paid homage to a variety of animals, and almost every city or district possessed its particular species to which special protection was extended. At Hermopolis and in other parts of Egypt the baboon was sacred, as well as the ibis, which typified the god Thoth. Cats were sacred both at Bubastis, where the cat-goddess, Bast, resided, and in various other districts. Crocodiles were very generally held in reverence, and several river fish were thus treated. The snake was much feared and reverenced ; and, as a pertinent example of this superstition, it may be mentioned that Ameno-phis III, the father of Akhnaton, placed a figure of the agathodemon serpent in a temple at Benha. The cobra was reverenced as the symbol of Uazet, the goddess of the Delta, and, first used as a royal emblem by the archaic kings of that country, it became the main emblem of sovereignty in Pharaonic times. It is unnecessary here to look more closely at this aspect of Egyptian religion ; and but a word need be said of the thousand demons and spirits which, together with the gods and the sacred animals, crowded the regions of the unknown. Many were the names which the magician might call upon in the hour of his need, and many were the awful forms which the soul of a man who had died was liable to meet. Osiris, the great god of the dead, was served by four such genii, and under his authority there sat no less than forty-two terrible demons whose business it was to judge the quavering soul. The numerous gates of the underworld were guarded by monsters whose names alone would strike terror into the heart, and the unfortunate soul had to repeat endless and peculiarly tedious formulæ before admittance was granted.

To minister to these hosts of heaven there had of necessity to be vast numbers of priests. At Thebes the priesthood of Amon formed an organisation of such power and wealth that the actions of the Pharaoh had largely come to be controlled by it. The High Priest of Amon-Ra was one of the most important personages in the land, and his immediate subordinates, the Second, Third, and Fourth Priests, as they were called, were usually nobles of the highest rank. The High Priest of Amon was at this period often Grand Vizir also, and thus combined the highest civil appointment with the highest sacerdotal office. The priesthood of Ra at Heliopolis, although of far less power than that of Amon, was also a body of great importance. The High Priest was known as " the Great One of Visions," and he was perhaps less of a politician and more of a priest than his Theban colleague. The High Priest of Ptah at Memphis was called "the Great Master Artificer," Ptah being the Vulcan of Egypt. He, however, and the many other high priests of the various gods, did not rank with the two great leaders of the Amon and the Ra priesthoods.

5. THUTMOSIS IV AND MUTEMUA

When Thutmosis IV ascended the throne he was confronted by a very serious political problem. The Heliopolitan priesthood at this time was chafing against the power of Amon, and was striving to restore the somewhat fallen prestige of its own god Ra, who in the far past had been the supreme deity of Egypt, but had now to play an annoying second to the Theban god. Thutmosis IV, as we shall presently be told by Akhnaton himself,[1] did not altogether

D   [1] Page 86

approve of the political character of the Amon priesthood, and it may have been due to this dissatisfaction that he undertook the repairing of the great sphinx at Gizeh, which was in the care of the priests of Heliopolis. The sphinx was thought to represent a combination of the Heliopolitan gods Horakhti, Khepera, Ra, and Atum, who have been mentioned above ; and according to a later tradition, Thutmosis IV had obtained the throne over the heads of his elder brothers through the mediation of the sphinx—that is to say, through that of the Heliopolitan priests. By them he was called " Son of Atum and Protector of Horakhte, . . . who purifies Heliopolis and satisfies Ra,"[1] and it seems that they looked to him to restore to them their lost power. The Pharaoh, however, was a physical weakling, whose small amount of energy was entirely expended upon his army, which he greatly loved, and which he led into Syria and into the Sudan. His brief reign of somewhat over eight years, from 1420 to 1411 B.C., marks but the indecisive beginnings of the struggle between Amon and Ra, which culminated in the early years of the reign of his grandson Akhnaton.

Some time before he came to the throne he had married a daughter of the King of Mitanni,

---

[1] The sphinx tablet.

a North-Syrian state which acted as a buffer between the Egyptian possessions in Syria and the hostile lands of Asia Minor and Mesopotamia, and which it was desirable, therefore, to placate by such a union. There is little doubt that this princess is to be identified with the Queen Mutemua, of whom several monuments exist, and who was the mother of Amenophis III, the son and successor of Thutmosis IV. A foreign element was thus introduced into the court which much altered its character, and led to numerous changes of a very radical nature. It may be that this Asiatic influence induced the Pharaoh to give further encouragement to the priests of Heliopolis. The god Atum, the aspect of Ra as the setting sun, was, as has been said, probably of common origin with Aton, who was largely worshipped in North Syria; and the foreign queen with her retinue may have therefore felt more sympathy with Heliopolis than with Thebes. Moreover, it was the Asiatic tendency to speculate in religious questions, and the doctrines of the priests of the northern god was more flexible and more adaptable to the thinker than was the stiff, formal creed of Amon. Thus, the foreign thought which had now been introduced into Egypt, and especially into the palace, may have contributed somewhat to the dissatisfaction with the state religion which becomes apparent during this reign.

Very little is known of the character of Thutmosis IV, and nothing which bears upon that of his grandson Akhnaton is to be ascertained. Although of feeble health and unmanly physique, he was a fond upholder of the martial dignity of Egypt. He delighted to honour the memory of those Pharaohs of the past who had achieved the greatest fame as warriors. Thus he restored the monuments of Thutmosis III, of Ahmose I, and of Sesostris III,[1] the three greatest military leaders of Egyptian history. As a decoration for his chariot there were scenes representing him trampling upon his foes ; and when he died many weapons of war were buried with him. Of Queen Mutemua's character nothing is known ; and the attention of the reader may at once be carried on to Akhnaton's maternal grandparents, the father and mother of Queen Tiy.

6. YUAA AND TUAU

Somewhere about the year 1470 B.C., while the great Thutmosis III was campaigning in Syria, the child was born who was destined to become the grandfather of the most remarkable of all the Pharaohs of Egypt. Neither the names of the parents nor the place of birth are known ;

[1] Of Thutmosis III. at Karnak, of Ahmose I. at Abydos, and of Sesostris III. at Amada.

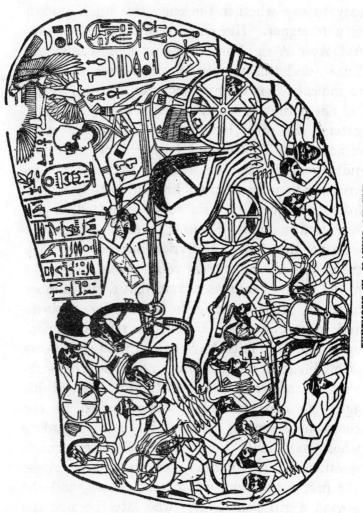

THUTMOSIS IV. SLAYING ASIATICS.

and the reader will presently find that it is not easy to say whether the child was an Egyptian or a foreigner. His name is written Aau, Aay, Aai, Ayu, A-aa, Yaa, Yau, and most commonly Yuaa ; and this variety of spelling seems rather to indicate that its pronunciation, being foreign, did not permit of a correct rendering in Egyptian letters. He must have been some twenty years of age when Thutmosis III died ; and thus it is quite possible that he was one of those Syrian princes whom the Pharaoh brought back to Egypt from the courts of Asia to be educated in the Egyptian manner. Some of these hostages who were not direct heirs to Syrian thrones may have taken up their permanent residence on the banks of the Nile, where it is certain that a fair number of their countrymen were settled for business and other purposes. During the reign of Amen ophis II, Yuaa must have passed the prime years of his life, and at that king's death he had probably reached about the forty-fifth year of his age. He had married a woman called by the common Egyptian name of Tuau, regarding whose nationality there is, therefore, not much question. Two children were born of the marriage, the first a boy who was named Aanen, and the second a girl named Tiy, who later became the great queen. Tiy was probably a little girl some two years old when Thutmosis IV came

to the throne, and as her parents both held
appointments at court, she must have presently
received those first impressions of royal luxury
which influenced her childhood and her whole
life.

At this time Yuaa held the sacerdotal office
of Priest of Min, one of the most ancient of the
Egyptian gods. Min, who had many of the
characteristics of, and was later identified with,
the Greek Pan, was worshipped at three or four
cities of Upper Egypt, and throughout the
Eastern Desert to the Red Sea coast. He was
the god of fecundity, fertility, generation, reproduction, and the like, in the human, animal,
and vegetable worlds. In his form of Min-Ra
he was a god of the sun, whose fertilising rays
made pregnant the whole earth. He was more
noble than the Greek Pan, and represented the
pristine desires of lawful reproduction in the
family, rather than the erotic instincts for which
the Greek god was famous. Were one to compare him with any of the gods of the countries
neighbouring to Egypt, he would be found to
have as much likeness to the above-mentioned
Adonis, who in North Syria was a god of vegeta-
tion, as to any other deity. This fact offers
food for some thought, for if Yuaa was a foreigner,
hailing, as may be supposed, from Syria, there
would have been no Egyptian god, except Atum,

to whose service he would have attached himself
so readily as to that of Min. Although a tribal
god, Min was not essentially the protector and
upholder of Egyptian rights and Egyptian
prejudices. He was, in one form or another,
universal; and he must have appealed to the
sense and the senses of Syrian and Egyptian
alike.

At this time, as we have seen, the priests of
Amon, whose wealth had brought corruption in
its train, were under the cloud of royal dis-
pleasure, and the court was beginning to display
a desire to rid itself of an influence which was
daily becoming less exalted. It may be that
Yuaa, upholding the doctrines of Min and of
Adonis, had some connection with this movement, for he was now a personage of considerable
importance at the palace. He may have already
held the title of Prince or Duke, by which he
is called in his funeral inscriptions; and one
may suppose that he was a favourite of the
young king, Thutmosis IV, and of his wife, Queen
Mutemua, whose blood was soon to unite with
his own in the person of Akhnaton. When
Thutmosis IV died at the age of twenty-six,
and his son Amonophis III, a boy of twelve
years of age, came to the throne, Yuaa was a
man of over fifty, and his little daughter Tiy
was a girl of marriageable age according to

Egyptian ideas, being about ten years old.[1]

The court at this time was more or less under the influence of the now Queen-Regent Mutemua and her advisers, for Amenophis III was still too young to be allowed to go entirely his own way; and amongst those advisers it seems evident that Yuaa was to be numbered. Now the boy-king had not been on the throne more than a year, if as much, when, with feasting and ceremony, he was married to Tiy; and Yuaa and Tuau became the proud parents-in-law of the Pharaoh.

It is necessary to consider the significance of the marriage. The royal pair were the merest children; and it is impossible to suppose that the marriage was not arranged for them by their guardians. If Amenophis at this early age had simply fallen in love with this girl, with whom probably he had been brought up, he, no doubt, would have insisted on marrying her, and she would have been placed in his *harîm*. But she became his Great Queen, was placed on the throne beside him, and received honours which no other queen of the most royal blood had ever received before. It is clear that the king's advisers would never have permitted this had Tiy been but the pretty daughter of a noble of the court. There must have been something

---

[1] These ages are discussed on pages 95 and 154 (note).

in her parentage which entitled her to these
honours and caused her to be chosen deliberately
as queen.

There are several possibilities. Tuau may
have had royal blood in her veins, and may have
been, for instance, the granddaughter of Thutmosis III, to whom she bears some likeness in
face. Queen Tiy is often called " Royal Daughter "
as well as " Royal Wife " ; and it is possible
that this is to be taken literally. In a letter
sent by Dushratta, King of Mitanni, to Akhnaton,
Tiy is called " my sister and thy mother " ; and
though it is possible that the word " sister " is
here used to indicate the general cousinship of
royalty, it is more probable that some real connection is meant, for other relationships, such
as " daughter," " wife," and " father-in-law,"
are precisely stated in the letter. Yuaa may
have been indirectly of royal Egyptian blood,
or he may have been, as we have seen, the off-
spring of some Syrian royal house, such as that
of Mitanni, related by marriage with the
Pharaoh ; and thus Tiy may have had some
distant claim to the throne, and Dushratta would
have had reason for calling her his sister. Queen
Tiy, however, has so often been called a foreigner
for reasons which have now been shown to be
quite erroneous that we must be cautious in
adopting any of these possibilities. It has been

stated that her face is North-Syrian in type,[1]
and, as the portrait upon which this statement is
based is, in all features except the nose, reminiscent of Yuaa, that noble would also resemble the
people of that country ; and in this connection
it must be remembered that the marriage of Tiy
and Amenophis took place under the regency
of Mutemua, herself probably a North-Syrian
princess. Be this as it may, however, the two
children, not yet in their 'teens, ruled Egypt
together, and Yuaa and Tuau stood behind the
throne to advise them.

Tuau now included amongst her titles those
of " Royal Handmaid," or lady-in-waiting, " the
favoured-one of Hathor," " the favourite of the
King," and " the Royal mother of the great wife
of the King," a title which may indicate that
she was of royal blood. Amongst the titles of
Yuaa one may mention those of " Master of the
Horse and Chariot-Captain of the King," " the
favourite, excellent above all favourites," and
" the mouth and ears of the King,"—that is to
say, his agent and adviser. He was a personage
of commanding presence, whose powerful character showed itself in his face. One must picture

[1] Petrie, History, ii. p. 183. The portrait upon which he bases
this statement, however, may be that of Akhnaton (fig. 115, p. 182).
The mouth and chin are extremely like those of Yuaa, as seen in his
mummy ; but again they both have a close resemblance to the head
of Amenophis III. (*idem*, fig. 120, p. 188). Of course, such evidence
is extremely frail, and must not be too much relied upon.

him now as a tall man, with a fine shock of white
hair ; a great hooked nose, like that of a Syrian ;
full, strong lips ; and a prominent, determined
jaw. He has the face of an ecclesiastic ; and
one feels, in looking at his well-preserved features,
that here perhaps may be found the originator
of the great religious movement which his
daughter and grandson carried into execution.

7. AMENOPHIS III AND HIS COURT

Besides Yuaa and Tuau and the Queen-
Dowager Mutemua, there was a certain noble,
named Amenophis-son-of-Hapu, who may have
exercised considerable influence upon the young
Pharaoh. So good and wise a man was he, that
in later times he was regarded almost as a divinity,
and his sayings were treasured from generation
to generation. It may be that he furthered the
cause of the Heliopolitan priesthood against
that of Amon ; and it is to be observed in this
connection that, in the inscription engraved
upon his statue, he refers to the Pharaoh as the
" heir of Atum " and the " first-born son of
Horakhti," those being the Heliopolitan gods.
When, presently, a daughter was born to Tiy,
who was named Setamon, this philosopher was
given the honorary post of " Steward " to the
princess ; while at the same time he filled the
office of a sort of Minister of Public Works, and

held various court appointments. At this
period, when religious speculation was beginning
to be freely indulged in, the influence of a " wise
man " of this character would necessarily be
great ; and should any of his sayings come to
light, they will perhaps be found to bear upon
the subject of the religious changes which were
now taking place. A late tradition tells us that
this Amenophis had warned the Pharaoh that
if he would see the true God he must drive from
his kingdom all impure persons ; and herein
one may perhaps observe some reference to the
corrupt priests of Amon, whose ejection from
their offices was daily becoming more necessary.
Josephus connects this tradition with the Exodus
of the Jews from Egypt, and it is possible that
the excavations of the Egypt Exploration Society
now (1922) being conducted on the site of the
city built by Akhnaton, may bring to light
information which will strengthen a now very
general feeling that the Exodus has some rela-
tion to the events which are described in the
following pages.

At the time of which we write Egypt still
remained at that height of power to which the
military skill of Thutmosis III had raised her.
The Kings of Palestine and Syria were tribu-
taries to the young Pharaoh ; the princes of the
sea-coast cities sent their yearly impost to

Thebes; Cyprus, Crete, and even the Greek islands, were Egyptianised; Sinai and the Red Sea coast as far south as Somaliland were included in the Pharaoh's dominions; and the negro tribes of the Sudan were his slaves. Egypt was indeed the greatest state in the world, and Thebes was a metropolis at which the ambassadors, the merchants, and the artisans from these various countries met together. Here they could look upon buildings undreamed of in their own lands, and could participate in luxuries unknown even in Babylon. The wealth of Egypt was so enormous that a foreign sovereign who wrote to the Pharaoh asking for gold mentioned that it could not be considered as anything more valuable than so much dust by an Egyptian. Golden vases in vast quantities adorned the table of the king and his nobles, and hundreds of golden vessels of different kinds were used in the temples.

The splendour and gaiety of the court at Thebes remind one of the tales from the Arabian Nights. One reads of banquets, of splendid festivals on the water, of jubilee celebrations, and of hunting parties. When the scenes depicted on the monuments are gathered together in the mind, and the ruins which are left are there reconstructed, a life of the most intense brilliancy is shown. This was rather a development of the period than a condition of things which had been derived from an earlier *régime*. The Egyptians had always been a happy, light-hearted people; but it was the conquests of Thutmosis III that had given them the security and the wealth to live as luxuriously as they pleased. The tendency of the nation was now to break away from the old, hardy traditions of the earlier periods of Egyptian history; and perhaps no other body, except the priesthood of Amon, held them down to ancient conventionalities. But while the king and his court made merry and amused themselves in sumptuous fashion, that god Amon and his representatives towered over them like some sombre bogie, holding them to a religion which they considered to be obsolete, and claiming its share of the royal wealth.

About the time of his marriage King Amenophis built a palace on the western bank of the Nile, on the edge of the desert under the Theban hills, and here Queen Tiy held her brilliant court. The palace was a light but roomy structure of brick and costly woods, exquisitely decorated with paintings on stucco, and embellished with delicate columns. Along one side ran a balcony on which were rugs and many-coloured cushions, and here the king and queen could sometimes be seen by their subjects. Gardens surrounded

the palace, almost at the gates of which rose
the splendid hills. On the eastern side of the
building the king later constructed a huge
pleasure-lake especially for the amusement of
Tiy. The mounds of earth which were thrown
up during its excavation were purposely formed
into irregular hills, these being covered with
trees and flowers; and here the queen floated
in her barge, which, in honour of the Heliopolitan
god, she called " Aton-gleams."

The name Aton perhaps had some remote
Syrian connection. The setting sun, as we have
seen, was called in Egypt Atum, which was
perhaps connected with the Asiatic Adon or
Adonis; and it is now that we first find the
word Aton introduced into Egypt as a synonym
of Ra-Horakhti-Khepera-Atum of Heliopolis,
though it had been used for long by the Egyptians
as the name of the actual orb or disc of the sun.
Presently we find that one of the Pharaoh's
regiments of soldiers is named after this god
Aton, and here and there the word now occurs
upon the monuments. Thus, gradually, the
court was bringing a new-named deity into
prominence, closely related to the gods of Heliopolis; and it may be supposed that the priesthood of Amon watched the development with
considerable perturbation. The Pharaoh himself
does not appear to have worried very considerably

with regard to these religious matters. He was, it seems, a man addicted to pleasure, whose interests lay as much in the hunting-field as in the palace. He loved to boast that during the first ten years of his reign he had slain 102 lions ; but as he was a mere boy when he first indulged in this form of sport, it is to be presumed that his nobles assisted him handsomely in the slaughter on each occasion. In one day he is reported to have killed fifty-six wild cattle, and a score more fell to him a few days later ; but here again one may suppose that the glory and not the deed was his.

In the fifth year of his reign he led an expedition into the Sudan to chastise some tribe which had rebelled, and he records with pride the slaughter which he had made. It is stated that these negroes " had been haughty, and great things were in their hearts ; but the fierce-eyed lion, this prince, he slew them by the command of Amon-Atum." It is interesting to notice that Atum is thus brought into equal prominence with Amon, and one may see from this the trend of public opinion.

At this time the Vizir, a certain Ptahmose, held also the office of High Priest of Amon ; but when he died he was not succeeded in his duties as Vizir by the new head of the Amon priesthood, as was to be expected. The Pharaoh

E

appointed a noble named Ramose as his prime minister, and thus separated the civil and the religious power : a step which again shows us something of the movement which was steadily diminishing the power of Amon.

Queen Tiy seems to have borne several daughters to the king, and it is possible that she had also presented him with a son. But, if this is so, he had died in early childhood, and no heir to the throne was now living. It may have been partly due to this fact that Amenophis, in the tenth year of his reign, married the Princess Kirgipa or Gilukhipa, daughter of the King of Mitanni, and probably niece of the Dowager-Queen Mutemua.[1] The princess came to Egypt in considerable state, bringing with her 317 ladies-in-waiting ; but she seems to have been thrust into the background by Tiy, who, even in the official record of the marriage, is called the king's chief wife. The marriage may have been purely political, as was that of Thutmosis IV ; and there is certainly no record of any children born to Gilukhipa. She and her ladies but added a further foreign element to the life of the palace, and swelled the numbers of those who had no sympathy with the old gods of Thebes.

It must have been somewhere about the year

---

[1] Breasted, Records, ii. 865, note h.

1390 B.C. that Tiy's aged father, Yuaa, died;
and Tuau soon followed him to the grave. They
were buried in a fine sepulchre in the Valley of
the Tombs of the Kings at Thebes; and if they
are not to be considered as royal, this will have
been the first time that persons not of royal
blood had been buried in a tomb of large size
in this valley. A quantity of funeral furniture
was placed around the splendid coffins in which
their mummies lay, and amongst this there were
a few objects which evidently had been presented
by the bereaved king and queen and by the
young princesses, Setamon and another whose
name is now lost. Yuaa and his wife had evi- *KiA?*
dently been much beloved at the court, and as
the parents of the reigning queen they had com-
manded the respect of all men. To us they are
remarkable as the grandparents of that great
teacher, Akhnaton, whose birth has now to be
recorded.

KiA MOTHER of TUT! ?

II

THE BIRTH AND EARLY YEARS
OF AKHNATON

1. THE BIRTH OF AKHNATON

IT has been seen that Queen Tiy presented several children to the king; but it was not until they had reigned some twenty-five years or so that the future monarch was born. As the years had passed the queen must have grown more and more anxious for a son, and many must have been the prayers she offered up that a male child might be vouchsafed to her. In Egypt at the present day the desire to bear a son holds dominion in the heart of every young woman; and those to whom this privilege has not been granted forsake the laws of the Prophet and still lay their passionate appeal before the old gods. The present writer was once asked by a young peasant to allow his wife to walk round the outer wall of an ancient temple, in order that she might perchance bear a male child thereafter; and on another occasion three young women were seen sliding down the plinth of an overturned statue of Rameses the Great for the same purpose. With similar emotion, though with greater intelligence, Queen Tiy must have turned in her grief from one god to another, promising them all manner of gifts if they would grant her desire. To Ra-Horakhti Aton she appears to have turned with the utmost confidence; and perhaps, as will presently be seen, she vowed that if a son were granted to her she would dedicate him to the service of that god.

It is probable that the little prince first saw the light in the royal palace at Thebes, which was situated on the edge of the desert at the foot of the western hills. It was, as has been said, an extensive building, lightly constructed and gaily decorated. The ceilings and pavements of its halls were fantastically painted with scenes of animal life; wild cattle ran through reedy swamps beneath the royal feet, and there many-coloured fish swam in the water; while overhead, flights of pigeons, white against a blue sky, passed across the hall, and wild duck hastened towards the open casements. Through curtained doorways one might obtain glimpses of the garden planted with flowers foreign to Egypt; and on the east of the palace shone the great pleasure-lake, surrounded by the trees of Asia.

In all the world there are few places more beautiful than the site of this palace. Here one may sit for many an hour watching the changing colours on the wonderful cliffs, the pink and the yellow of the rocks standing out from the blue and the purple of the deep shadows. In the fields which now surround the ruined palace, where the royal gardens were laid out, one obtains an impression of colour, of beauty, and of gaiety —if it can be so expressed—which is not easily equalled. The continuous sunshine and the bracing wind render one intensely awake to natural joys; and here, indeed, was a fitting birthplace, one feels, for a king who taught his people to study the beauties of nature.

2. THE RISE OF ATON

The little prince was named Amenhotep,[1] or, as the later Greeks transcribed it, Amenophis "the Peace-of-Amon," after his father; but though the supremacy of Amon was thus acknowledged, the Heliopolitan deity appears to have been considered as the protector of the young boy. While the luxurious court rejoiced at the birth of their future king, one feels that the ancient priesthood of Amon-Ra must have looked askance at the baby who was destined one day to be their master. This priesthood

---

[1] He took the name Akhnaton in about the sixth year of his reign.

still demanded implicit obedience to its stiff and ancient conventions, and it refused to recognise the growing tendency towards religious speculation.

Probably stronger measures would have been taken by it to resist the growing power of Ra-Horakhti, had it not been for the fact that Ra was also a form of Amon, and had been identified with him under the name of Amon-Ra. The god Amon was originally but the local deity of Thebes ; and, when the Theban Pharaohs of the Eighteenth Dynasty had elevated him to the position of the state god of all Egypt, they made him acceptable to the various provinces, as we have seen, by pointing to his identification with Ra, the sun-god, who, under one form or another, found a place in every temple and held high rank in every variety of mythology. As Amon-Ra he was able to be appreciated by the sun-worshippers of Syria and by those of Nubia, for there were few races who would not do homage to the great giver of warmth and light.

It is possible that those more thoughtful members of the court who were quietly attempting to undermine the influence of the priesthood of Amon, and who were beginning to carry into execution the schemes of emancipation which we have already noticed, now endeavoured to strip Amon of his association with the sun ; for that identity was really his simple claim to acceptance by any but Thebans. The priesthood, on their part, it may be supposed, drew as much attention as possible to the connection of their deity with Ra ; for they knew that none but the Heliopolitan god could be advanced with success as a rival of Amon by those who desired to overthrow the Theban god. Thus one finds that the High Priest of Ra at Heliopolis was given, and was perhaps obliged to accept, the honorary office of Second Priest of Amon at Thebes,[1] which at once placed him under the thumb of the Theban High Priest. The propounders of the new thought, however, met this move by bringing into greater prominence the claims, not of Ra-Horakhti, but of Aton, which was merely a more elusive form of the sun-god. The priesthood of Amon had always checked the individual growth of Ra-Horakhti by regarding him simply as an aspect of Ra, and hence of Amon-Ra. One of the essential features of the new movement was the regarding of Ra as an aspect of Ra-Horakhti, and the calling of Ra-Horakhti by the uncontaminated name of Aton. Aton, in fact, was originally introduced into the matter largely for the purpose of preventing any identification between Amon-Ra and Ra-Horakhti. Soon the name

[1] His statue is at Turin. See also Erman, " Life in Ancient Egypt," p. 297.

of Aton, entirely supplanting that of Atum, was heard with some frequency at Thebes and elsewhere, but always, it must be remembered, as another word for Ra-Horakhti.

The desire of the court for a change in religion is understandable. The cult of the god Amon, as has been said, was so hedged about with conventionalities that free thought was impossible. We have seen, however, that the upper classes were passing through a phase of religious speculation, and they were ready to revolt against the domination of a priesthood which forbade criticism. The worship of the intangible power of the sun, under the name of Aton, offered endless possibilities for the exercise of those tendencies towards the abstract which were now beginning to be felt all over the civilised world. This was man's first age of philosophical thought, and for the first time in history the gods were being endued with ideal qualities.

Apart from all questions of religion, the priesthood of Amon had obtained such power and wealth that it was a very serious menace to the dignity of the throne. The great organisation which had its headquarters at Karnak had become an incubus which weighed heavily upon the state. For political reasons alone, therefore, it was desirable to push the priests of Heliopolis into a more prominent position.

There was, moreover, a third consideration. The Aton, with which Ra and Ra-Horakhti were now being identified, being a solar deity of universal and not local aspect, was likely to make a wide appeal. Thus the propounders of the new doctrines must have dreamt of an Egypto-Syrian empire bound together by the ties of a common religion. With one god understood and worshipped from the cataracts of the Nile to the distant Euphrates, what power could destroy the empire ?

In passing, an interesting suggestion may here be made, though in our present paucity of information, the subject cannot be pursued very far. This Aton worship as will be seen in the following pages, developed into an exalted monotheism, and it originated in Heliopolis. Now Heliopolis is the ancient On, where Moses learnt all " the wisdom of the Egyptians " ; and thus there may be some connection between the Jewish faith and that of the Aton.

3. THE POWER OF QUEEN TIY

In Amenophis III one may see the lazy, speculative Oriental, too opinionated and too vain to bear with the stiff routine of his fathers, and yet too lacking in energy to formulate a new religion. On the other hand, there is every

reason to suppose that Queen Tiy possessed the
ability to impress the claims of the new thought
upon her husband's mind, and gradually to turn
his eyes, and those of the court, away from the
sombre worship of Amon into the direction of
the brilliant cult of the sun. Those who have
travelled in Egypt will realise how completely
the land is dominated by the sun. The blue
skies, the shining rocks, the golden desert, the
verdant fields, all seem to cry out for joy of the
sunshine. The extraordinary energy which one
may feel in Egypt at sunrise, and the deep
melancholy which sometimes accompanies the
red nightfall, must have been felt by Tiy also
in her palace at Thebes.

As the years passed, the power and influence
of Queen Tiy increased; and now that she had
borne a son to the king there was added to her
great position as royal wife the equally great
rôle of royal mother. Never before had a queen
been so freely represented on all the king's monuments, nor had so fine a series of titles been given
before to the wife of a Pharaoh. At Serdênga,
far up in the Sudan, her husband erected a temple
for her; and in distant Sinai a beautiful portrait
head of her was recently found. All visitors to
Thebes have seen her figure by the side of the
legs of the two great colossi at the edge of the
Western Desert; and the huge statues of herself

and her husband, now in the Cairo Museum, will have been seen by those who have visited that collection. Of Gilukhipa,[1] however, and the king's other wives, one hears nothing at all : Queen Tiy relegated them to the background almost before their marriage ceremonies were over.

By the time that Amenophis III had reigned for thirty years or so, he had ceased to give much attention to state affairs, and the power had almost entirely passed into the capable hands of Tiy. Already an influence, which we may presume to have been to a large extent hers, was being felt in many directions : Ra-Horakhti and Aton were being brought into the foreground, a tone of thought which can hardly be regarded as purely Egyptian was being developed, the art was undergoing modifications and had risen to a pitch of excellence never attained before or after. The exquisite low-reliefs of the end of the reign of Amenophis III— for example, those to be seen at Thebes in the tombs of Khaemhet and of Ramose,[2] both of which are definitely dated to the close of the reign—stir one almost as do the works of the early Florentine masters. There is an elusive grace in the dainty figures there sculptured, which, through another medium and under other laws

[1] Page 34.
[2] Discovered by the present writer whilst repairing this tomb.

of convention, cause them to appeal with the same force of indefinable sweetness as do the figures in the works of Filipino Lippi and Botticelli. In the mass of Egyptian painting and sculpture of secondary importance such gems as these have been overlooked and have not been appreciated by the public ; but the present writer ventures to think that some day they will set the heart of all art-lovers dancing as danced those of Queen Tiy's great masters.

The court in which the little prince passed his earliest years was more brilliant than ever it had been before, and Queen Tiy presided over scenes of indescribable splendour. Amenophis III. has been truly called " the Magnificent " ; and at no period, save that of Thutmosis III, were the royal treasuries so full or the nobles so wealthy. Out of a pageant of festivities, from amidst the noise of song and laughter, the little sad-eyed prince first emerges on to the stage of history, led by the hand of Queen Tiy ; but as he appears before us, above the clink of the golden wine-bowls, above the sound of the timbrels, one seems to hear the lilt of a more simple song, and the peaceful singing of a lark.

4. AKHNATON'S MARRIAGES

During the last years of his reign the Pharaoh, although well under fifty years of age, seems to have suffered from permanent ill-health.[1] On two occasions the King of Mitanni sent to Egypt a miracle-working statue of the goddess Ishtar, apparently in the hope that Amenophis might be cured of his illness by it. It is probable that the king had never been a very strong man. Having been born when his father—himself extremely delicate—was but a child, he had had little chance of enjoying a robust middle-age, and he passed on to his children this inherent weakness. One hears no more of his daughters,[2] whom we have seen mourning for their grandparents Yuaa and Tuau, and there is some likelihood that they died young. The little Prince Amenophis was already developing constitutional weaknesses which rendered his life very precarious. His skull was misshapen, and he must have been subject to occasional epileptic fits. And now Queen Tiy gave birth to a daughter, who was named Baketaton in honour of the new god, and who seems to have lived less than a score of years, since nothing more is heard of her after her twelfth or thirteenth year.

As Amenophis III, at the age of forty-eight or forty-nine, felt his end approaching, he must

[1] His mummy is that of a man of not more than fifty.

[2] The wise man Amenophis-son-of-Hapu was steward of Princess Setamon s estate, but this may have been previous to her mention in her grandparents' tomb.

have experienced considerable anxiety in regard
to the succession. Here was his only son—now
a boy of eleven or twelve years of age—in so sad
a state of health that he could not be expected
to live to manhood, and in the event of his
death the throne would be without an occupant
in the direct line. Obviously it was necessary
that he should be married soon, in order that
he might become a father as early as that was
naturally possible. Amenophis III himself had
been married to Tiy when he was about twelve
years of age, and his father Thutmosis IV had
likewise been married at that early age.[1] The
little Prince Amenophis should, therefore, also
be given a wife at once ; and the Pharaoh now
began to look around for a suitable consort for
him. He had heard that Dushratta, King of
Mitanni, had a small daughter who was said
to be a comely maiden ; and there were many
political reasons for proposing the union.
Mitanni was, as we have seen, the buffer state
between the Pharaoh's Syrian possessions and
the lands of the Hittites and of the Mesopota-
mians. Thutmosis IV had asked a bride from
Mitanni, and Amenophis III himself had obtained
Gilukhipa from thence, if not Queen Tiy also ;
both these being probably political matches,
designed for the welfare of the Syrian empire.

[1] Page 95.

The Pharaoh therefore decided upon this marriage for his sickly son, and sent an embassy to Dushratta to negotiate the union between these two children.

The reply of Dushratta has, fortunately, been preserved to us. The Mitannian king acknowledges the arrival of the envoy, and is much rejoiced at this further binding together of the two countries. In a subsequent letter it is evident that the princess has already been sent to Egypt, and we are led to suppose that Prince Amenophis has at once been married to her. The little princess was named Tadukhipa, but after her arrival in Egypt we hear no more of her, and it is probable that she died at an early age.

Prince Amenophis was then, it seems, married to a young Egyptian girl named Nefertiti, who ultimately became his queen. She was the daughter of a noble named Ay, who later was always known as " Father-in-law of the King," a title which, until Dr. Borehardt pointed out its true meaning, had always been mistranslated " Divine Father " and regarded as of religious significance. This Ay was married to a lady called Ty, but Nefertiti seems to have been the daughter of an earlier wife ; for Ty is spoken of as " great nurse and nourisher " of Nefertiti and not as her mother.

It has generally been thought that Nefertiti and Tadukhipa were to be identified and that Ay and Ty were the foster parents of this foreign princess ; but there is far more reason to suppose that the fact is as here stated, and that Nefertiti was an Egyptian girl who was married to the Prince after the death of Tadukhipa. This is confirmed by the finding of a portrait head of a queen, which, by the style of the work and the shape of the crown, can only be that of Nefertiti, and yet which shows a woman of marked Egyptian and not of foreign physiognomy.[1] Nefertiti was probably two or three years younger than the Prince, for her first child was not born until nearly five years later, and Egyptian girls are usually mothers by the age of thirteen or fourteen.

Soon after these events the court was thrown into mourning by the death of Amenophis " the Magnificent," which occurred in the thirty-sixth year of his reign. Queen Tiy at once assumed control of state affairs on behalf of her twelve or thirteen-year-old son, who as Amenophis IV now ascended the throne of the Pharaohs, with Nefertiti as his queen.

---

[1] This head is now in the Berlin Museum, and photographs have not yet been issued. In the tomb made for this Ay at El Amarna there is an inscription in which he speaks of the Queen and prays that she may remain by Akhnaton's side for ever and ever. He speaks of her beauty, her sweet voice, her " two beautiful hands," and so on.

F

5. THE ACCESSION OF AKHNATON

On coming to the throne the young king fixed his titulary in the following manner :—

> Mighty Bull, Lofty of Plumes ; Favourite of the Two Goddesses, Great in Kingship in Karnak; Golden Hawk, Wearer of Diadems in the Southern Heliopolis ; King of Upper and Lower Egypt, Beautiful-is-the-Being-of-Ra, the Only-One-of-Ra ; Son of the Sun, Peace-of-Amon (Amenophis), Divine Ruler of Thebes ; Great in Duration, Living for Ever and Ever, Beloved of Amon-Ra, Lord of Heaven.

These titles were drawn up on more or less prescribed lines, and conformed to the old custom of the Pharaohs. Like his ancestors, he was called " Beloved of Amon-Ra," although, as we have seen, the power of that god was already much undermined. To counterbalance this reference to the god of Thebes, however, one finds the surprising title—

> High Priest of Ra-Horakhti, rejoicing in the horizon in his name, " Heat-which-is-in-Aton."

Let the boy be said to be beloved of Amon-Ra till the walls of Thebes reverberate with the cry ; let Amon-Ra be called Lord of Heaven till the priestly heralds can shout no more : the doom of the god of Thebes cannot now be averted, for the reigning Pharaoh is dedicated to another god. It is obvious that a boy of twelve or thirteen years of age could not himself have claimed the

office of the High Priest of Ra-Horakhti. Queen
Tiy and her advisers must have deliberately
endowed the youthful king with this office,
largely in order to set the seal upon the fate of
Amon. There were, perhaps, other reasons why
this remarkable step was decided upon. It may
be, as has been said, that the queen, before the
birth of her son, had vowed him to Ra-Horakhti.
Again, the boy was epileptic, was subject to
hallucinations; and it may be that while in
this condition he had seen visions or uttered
words which led his mother to believe him to
be the chosen one of the Heliopolitan god, whose
name the prince must have been constantly
hearing. In a palace where the mystical " Heat-
which-is-in-Aton," which was the new elabora-
tion of the god's name, was being daily invoked,
and where the youthful master of Egypt was
occasionally falling into what appeared to be
holy frenzy, it is not unlikely that the rising
deity would be connected with the eccentricities
of the young Pharaoh. The High Priest of
Ra-Horakhti was always called " The Great of
Visions," and was thus essentially a visionary
prophet either by nature or by circumstance;
and the unfortunate boy's physical condition
may have been turned, thus, to account in the
struggle against Amon-Ra.

One may imagine now the Pharaoh as a pale,

sickly youth. His head seemed too large for
his body ; his eyelids were heavy ; his eyes were
eloquent of dreams. His features were delicately
moulded, and his mouth, in spite of a somewhat
protruding lower jaw, is reminiscent of the best
of the art of Rossetti. He seems to have been
a quiet, studious boy, whose thoughts wandered
in fair places, searching for that happiness which
his physical condition had denied to him. His
nature was gentle ; his young heart overflowed
with love. He delighted, it would seem, to walk
in the gardens of the palace, to hear the birds
singing, to watch the fish in the lake, to smell the
flowers, to follow butterflies, to warm his small
bones in the sunshine. Already he was sometimes called " Lord of the Breath of Sweetness " ; [1]
and already, perhaps, he was so much beloved
by his subjects that their adherence to him
through the rough places of his future life was
assured. For the first years of his reign he was,
of course, entirely under the regency of his
mother. Dushratta, the King of Mitanni, writing
to congratulate the boy on his accession, addressed
himself to Queen Tiy, as though he thought
the king would hardly yet be able to understand
a letter ; and in a later communication he asks
the Pharaoh to inquire of his mother as to certain

[1] Scarabs of the early period are sometimes inscribed *Neb-nef-nezem*
which has this meaning.

matters of international policy. But although
so young, the king was wise beyond his years,
as the reader will presently see.

6. THE FIRST YEARS OF AKHNATON'S REIGN

In a subsequent chapter it will be the writer's
purpose to show to what heights of ideal thought,
and to what profundities of religious and moral
philosophy, this boy, in the years of his early
manhood, attained ; and it will but enhance our
respect for his abilities when he reached maturity,
if we find in his early training all manner of
shortcomings. The beautiful doctrines of the
religion with which this Pharaoh's name is identified were productions of his later days ; and until
he was at least seventeen or eighteen years of
age neither his exalted monotheism nor any of
his future principles were really apparent. Some
time after the eighth year of his reign one finds
that he had evolved a religion so pure that one
must compare it with Christianity in order to
discover its faults ; and the reader will presently
see that the superb theology was not derived
from his education.

One of the first acts of the king's reign, under-
taken at the desire of Queen Tiy or of the royal
advisers, was the completion of a temple to

Ra-Horakhti Aton at Karnak,[1] which was probably begun by Amenophis III. This was in no way an insult to Amon, for Thutmosis III and other Pharaohs had dedicated temples at Karnak to gods other than Amon. The priesthood of Amon-Ra recognised the existence of the many deities of Egypt, and gave them their place in the constitution of heaven, reserving for their own god the title of " King of the Gods." There was a temple of Ptah here ; there were shrines set apart for the worship of Min ; and other gods, unconnected with Amon, were here accommodated. The priests of Amon-Ra thus could not offer any serious objection to the project. The building[2] was constructed of sandstone, and therefore various officials were dispatched to the great quarries of Gebel Silsileh, which lie on the river between Edfu and Kom Ombo, and to those near Esneh. Large tablets were there carved upon the cliffs towards the close of the work, and on them the figure of the Pharaoh was represented worshipping Amon, who was thus still the state god. Above the king's figure, however, the disk of the sun is

[1] The date of this work is not exactly known, but on a fragment now in Berlin there are traces of the erased cartouch of Amenophis III, over which the name of Akhnaton has been imposed.

[2] The word *benben*, " shrine," has the hieroglyph of an obelisk at the end of it, which has led to some mistranslations. Perhaps the temple was built somewhat on the plan of that at Abusêr, where an obelisk stood in an open court.

seen, and from it a number of lines, representing rays, project downwards towards the royal figure. These rays terminate in hands, which thus seem to be distributing the " heat-which-is-in-Aton " around the Pharaoh. This is the first representation of the afterwards famous symbol of the religion of Aton, and it is significant that it should make its appearance in a scene representing the worship of Amon.

As early as the time of the Pyramid Texts we read of the " *arm* of the sun-beams " ; but this symbol of the new religion was novel, and appears to have been designed and invented by the young king himself.

The king is called the High Priest of Ra-Horakhti ; but the title " Living in truth," which he took to himself in later years, and which had reference to the religion of Aton which he was soon to evolve, does not yet appear.

A large number of fragments from this shrine have been discovered, and on these one sees references to the gods Horus, Set, Wepwat, and others. The king is still called by the name Amenophis, which was later banned, and the names of Aton, afterwards always written within the royal ovals or cartouches, are still lacking in that distinction. The temple was called " Aton-is-found-in-the-House-of-Aton," a curious

name of which the meaning is not clear.[1]
A certain official named Hataay was "Scribe
and Overseer of the Granary of the House of
the Aton," by which this temple is probably
meant ; and in the tomb of Ramose a reference
is made to the building by its full name, and
a picture of it is given, but otherwise one knows
little about it. The rapidity with which it was
desired to be set up is shown by the fact that
the great, well-trimmed blocks of stone usually
employed in the construction of sacred buildings
were largely dispensed with, and only small
easily-handled blocks were used. The imper-
fections in the building were then hidden by
a judicious use of plaster and cement, and thus
the walls were smoothed for the reception of
the reliefs. The quarter in which the temple
stood was now called " Brightness of Aton the
Great," and Thebes received the new name of
" City of the Brightness of Aton."

There are two other monuments which date
from these early years of the king's reign : both
are tombs of great nobles. At this period one
of the greatest personages in the land was the
above-mentioned Ramose, the Vizir of Upper
Egypt. This official was now engaged in constructing and decorating a magnificent sepulchre
for himself in the Theban necropolis. In the

[1] It is possible that " found " is a mistranslation.

great hall of this tomb the artists were busy
preparing the beautiful sculptures and paintings
which were to cover the walls, and ere half their
work was finished they set themselves to the
making of a fine figure of Amenophis IV seated
upon his throne, with the goddess Maat standing
behind him. The scene was probably executed
a few months before the making of the tablets
at the quarries. The sun's rays do not appear,
and the work was carried out strictly according
to the canons of art obtaining during the last
years of Amenophis III and the first of his son.
But hardly had the figures been finished before
the order came that the Aton rays had to be
included, and certain changes in the art had to
be recognised; and therefore the artists set
to work upon another figure of the king standing
under these many-handed beams of "heat,"
and now accompanied by his as yet childless wife.
The two scenes may be seen by visitors to Thebes
standing side by side, and nowhere may the
contrast between the old order of things and
the new be so clearly observed.

While Ramose was providing a tomb for
himself at Thebes, another great noble named
Horemheb, who ultimately usurped the throne,
was constructing his sepulchre at Sakkârah, the
Memphite necropolis near Cairo. Horemheb was
commander-in-chief of the army, and in his

tomb some superb reliefs are carved showing him receiving rewards in that capacity from the king. Some of the scenes represent the arrival of Asiatic refugees in Egypt, who ask to be allowed to take up their abode on the banks of the Nile, and the figures of these foreigners rank amongst the finest specimens of Egyptian art. In the inscriptions, Horemheb, who is supposed to be ·addressing the king, states that the Pharaoh owes his throne to Amon,[1] but yet we see that the figure of the king is drawn in that style of art which is typical of the new religion.[2]

In the same style the new king is shown upon some damaged reliefs in the northern colonnade of the temple of Luxor, a building begun by Amenophis III and finished by Tutankhamen and Horemheb.

7. THE NEW ART

This sudden change in the style of the reliefs which we have observed in these two tombs and on the quarry tablets seems to be attributable to about the fourth year of the king's reign. The reliefs which were now carved upon the walls of the new temple of Ra-Horakhti at

[1] Thus corresponding to the Silsileh quarry tablet, where Amon is worshipped.

[2] This tomb of Horemheb seems to have been begun and finished in the early years of Akhnaton's reign, to have been left alone during the remainder of the reign, and to have received the addition

Karnak show us a style of art quite different from that of the king's early years. The figure of the Pharaoh, which the artists in the tomb of Ramose represented as standing below the newly-invented sun's rays, is entirely different from the earlier figure there executed. The young Pharaoh whom we see in the tomb of Horemheb and on the quarry tablets is represented according to canons of art entirely different from those existing at the king's accession.

In the drawing of the human figure, and especially that of the Pharaoh, there are three very distinct characteristics in this new style of art. Firstly, as to the head: the skull is elongated; the chin, as seen in profile, is drawn as though it were sharply pointed; the flesh under the jaw is skimped, thus giving an upward turn to the line; and the neck is represented as being long and thin. Secondly, the stomach is made to obtrude itself upon the attention by being drawn as though from an ungainly model. And thirdly, the hips and thighs are abnormally large, though from the knee downwards the legs are of more natural size. This

of doorposts (see note on p. 235) after the death of Akhnaton. Frag ments of the tomb are now divided between Leiden, Bologna, Vienna, Alexandria, and Cairo; and it would seem that all except those in the Cairo museum (the doorposts) are from the earlier period. The titles on the Cairo fragments are far more elaborate than those on the others. See Breasted, Records, iii. 1 ff.

distortion of human anatomy is marked in a lesser degree in all the lines of the body ; and the whole figure becomes a startling type of an art which seems at first to have sprung fully developed from the brain of the boy-Pharaoh or from one of the eccentrics of the court.

The king was now seventeen years old, and seems to have been extraordinarily mature for his age. It may be that he had objected to be represented in the conventional manner, and had told his artists to draw him as he was. The elongated skull, the pointed chin, and even, perhaps, the protruding paunch, may thus have originated. But the ungainly thighs could only be accounted for by some radical deformity in the royal model, and yet that he was a fairly well-made man in this respect his bones most clearly show.

Purely tentatively a suggestion may here be offered to account for this peculiar treatment of the human body. It is probable that the king had now, in a boyish way, become deeply interested in the religious contest which was beginning to be waged between Amon-Ra and Ra-Horakhti Aton. Having listened to the arguments on both sides, it may have occurred to him to study for himself the ancient documents and inscriptions bearing on the matter. In so doing, he would have found that Amon had become the state god only some few hundred years before his own time, and that previous to his ascent to this important position, previous even to the earliest mention of his name, Ra-Horakhti had been supreme. Carrying his inquiries back, past the days of the pyramid-kings to the archaic Pharaohs who reigned at the dim beginnings of things, he would still have found the Heliopolitan god worshipped. One of the Pharaohs' most cherished titles was "Son of the Sun," which, as we have seen, had been borne by each successive sovereign since the days of the Fifth Dynasty, whose kings claimed descent from Ra himself. Such studies would inevitably bring two matters into prominence : firstly, that Amon was, after all, but a usurper ; and, secondly, that as Pharaoh he was the descendant of Ra-Horakhti, and was that god's representative on earth.

On these grounds, more than on any others, all things connected with Amon would become distasteful to him. He was too young to understand fully which of the two religions was the better morally or theologically ; but he was old enough to be moved by the romance of history, and to feel that those great, shadowy Pharaohs who lived when the world was young, and who at the dawn of events worshipped the sun, were the truest and best examples for him to follow. They were his ancestors, and as they were the sons of Ra, so he, too, was the proud descendant of that great god. In his veins there ran the blood of the sun, that "heat-which-is-in-Aton" pulsed through and through him; and the more he read in those old documents the more he may have been stirred by the glory of that distant past when men worshipped the god whose rights Amon had usurped. Now the canons of art were regarded as a distinctly religious institution, and the methods of treating the human figure then in vogue had in the first place the sanction of the priesthood of Amon; and few things would be more upsetting to their *régime* than the abandoning of these canons. This was probably recognised by those who were furthering the cause of Ra-Horakhti, and the young king may have been assisted and encouraged in his views. Presently it may have been brought home to him that, since he was thus the representative of those archaic kings and the High Priest of their god, it was fitting that the canons acknowledged by those far-off ancestors should be recognised by him. Here, then, he would both please his own romantic fancy and deal a blow at the Amon priesthood by banning the art which they upheld, and by infusing into the sculptures and paintings of his time something of the spirit of the most ancient art of Egypt.

Amon
OR
AMEN
OR
AHMEN

In the old temples of Heliopolis and elsewhere a few relics of that period, no doubt, were still preserved ; and the king was thus able to study the wood and slate carvings and the ivory figures of archaic times. We of the present day can also study such figures, a few specimens having been brought to light by modern excavators ; and the similarity between the treatment of the human body in this archaic art and the new art of Akhnaton at once becomes apparent. In the accompanying illustrations some archaic figures are shown, and one may perhaps see in them the origin of the idiosyncrasies of the new school. Here and in all representations of archaic men one sees the elongated skull so characteristic of the king's style ; in the ivory figure of an archaic Pharaoh one sees the well-known droop of Akhnaton's head and his pointed chin ; in the clay and ivory figures is the prominent stomach ; and here also, most apparent of all, are the unaccountably large thighs and ponderous hips.

Akhnaton's art might thus be said to be a kind of renaissance—a return to the classical period of archaic days ; the underlying motive of this return being the desire to lay emphasis upon the king's character as the representative of that most ancient of all gods, Ra-Horakhti.

Another feature of the new religion now

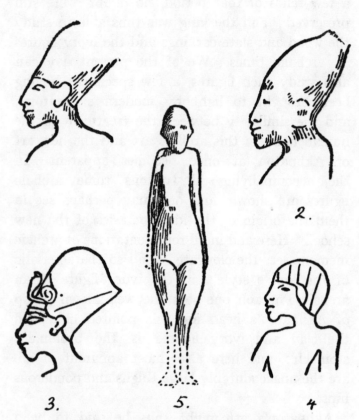

THE ART OF AKHNATON COMPARED WITH ARCHAIC ART.

1. The head of Akhnaton.   From a contemporary drawing.
2. The head of a king.   From an archaic statuette found by Professor Petrie at Abydos.
3. The head of Akhnaton.   From a contemporary drawing.
4. The head of a prince.   From an archaic tablet found by Professor Petrie at Abydos.
5. An archaic statuette found by Professor Petrie at Diospolis, showing the large thighs found in the art of Akhnaton.

becomes apparent. In the worship of Ra-Horakhti Aton there was an endeavour to do honour to the Pharaoh as the son of the sun, and to the god as the founder of the royal line. Tradition stated that Ra or Ra-Horakhti had once reigned upon earth, and that his spirit had passed from Pharaoh to Pharaoh. This god was thus the only true King of Heaven, and Amon was but a usurper of much more recent date. It was for this reason that the names of the new god were placed within royal cartouches; and for this reason the king was so careful to call Ra-Horakhti his " father," and to name him " god and king." For this reason also Akhnaton often wore the crown of Lower Egypt which was used at Heliopolis, but hardly ever the crown of Upper Egypt,[1] which history told him did not exist when Ra ruled on earth.[2]

Apart from the representation of the human form, the new art is chiefly characterised by its freedom of poses. An attempt is made to break away from tradition, and a desire is shown to have done with the conventions of the age. Never before had the artists caught the swing of a walk, the relaxation of a seated figure, so

[1] He is shown wearing the Upper Egyptian crown on a stela in the Cairo Museum, and on a fragment belonging to Col. Anderson, now loaned to the Ashmolean Museum, Oxford.

[2] We know from the " Palermo stone " that the kingdom of Lower Egypt was much more ancient than that of Upper Egypt.

G

well or so truthfully. Sculpture in the round now reached a height of perfection which places it above all but the art of the Greeks in the old world; and there is a grace and naturalness in the low reliefs which command one's admiration. A portrait head of Queen Nefertiti is a work of art which must be ranked with the world's greatest masterpieces. It was found by German excavators at El Amarna and is now in the Berlin Museum; but a photograph has not yet been published or issued.

There are only two artists of the period who are known by name.[1] The one was a certain Auta, who is represented in a relief dating from some eight years after the change in the art had taken place. It is a significant fact that this personage held the post of master-artist to Queen Tiy; and it is possible that in him and his patron we have the originators of the movement. The king, however, was now old enough to take an active interest in such matters; and the other artist who is known by name, a certain Bek, definitely states that the king himself taught him. Thus there is reason to suppose that the young Pharaoh's own hand is to be traced in the new canons, although they were instituted when he was but fifteen years old.

[1] A third artist, Thutmose, is also known, but he flourished towards the end of the reign. See page 180.

8. THE NEW RELIGION DEVELOPS

There is an interesting record, apparently dating from about this period, which is to be seen upon the rocks near the breccia quarries of Wady Hammamât. Here there are three cartouches standing upon two *neb* signs, symbolic of sovereignty, and above them is the disk and rays of the new religion. One of these cartouches, surrounded by the tall feathers worn by the queens of this period, contains a very short name, which can only be that of Queen Tiy.[1] The other two cartouches contain the names Amenophis (IV) and the Pharaoh's second designation. Thus we see that after the new religious symbol had been introduced, and just before the king took the name of " Akhnaton," Queen Tiy still held equal royal rank with him, and was evidently Regent.

During the seventeenth to the nineteenth years of his age the king seems to have devoted a considerable amount of time and thought to the changes which were taking place. With the enthusiasm of youth he threw himself into the new movement, and one may suppose that it

[1] In later times the name of Tiy and the Pharaoh's second name were erased, but the name Amenophis was not damaged. A facsimile copy was made on the spot by the present writer in correction of a previous copy made by Golénischeff. It is published in his " Travels in the Upper Egyptian Deserts " (Blackwood).

required all Queen Tiy's tact and diplomacy to keep him from offending his country by some rash action against the priesthood of Amon. Those priests were by no means reconciled to the king's devotion to Ra-Horakhti; and although he still nominally served the Theban god, they felt that every day he was becoming more estranged from that deity. No doubt there were many passages of arms between the High Priest of Amon-Ra and this royal High Priest of the sun, young as he was. The new art, upsetting all the old religious conventions, was distasteful to the priests; the new religious thought did not conform to their stereotyped doctrines; and much that the king said must have been absolutely heretical to their ears. The tide of thought, now directed in so eager and boyishly unreserved a manner, was sweeping them from their feet, and they knew not whither they were being carried.

The court officials blindly followed their young king, and to every word which he spoke they listened attentively. Sometimes the thoughts which he voiced came direct from the mazes of his own mind; sometimes perhaps he repeated the utterances of his deep-thinking mother; and sometimes there may have passed from his lips the pearls of wisdom which he had gleaned from the wise men of his court. At his behest

the dreamers of Asia had probably related to him their visions ; the philosophers had made pregnant his mind with the mystery of knowledge ; the poets had sung to him harp-songs in which echoed the beliefs of the elder days ; the priests of strange gods had submitted to him the creeds of strange people. He had not walked in the shadow of the cedars of Lebanon, nor had he ascended the Syrian hills ; but nevertheless the hymns of Adonis and the chants of Baal were probably as familiar to him as were the solemn chants of Amon-Ra. At the cosmopolitan court of Thebes men of all nations were assembled. The hills of Crete, the gardens of Persia, the incense-groves of Araby, added their philosophies to his dreams, and the haunting lips of Babylon whispered to him mysteries of far-off days. From Sardinia, Sicily, and Cyprus there must have come to him the doctrines of those who had business in great waters ; and Libya and Ethiopia disclosed their creeds to his eager ears. The fertile brain of the Pharaoh, it seems probable, was thus sown at an early age with the seed of all that was wonderful in the world of thought.

It must always be remembered that the king had much foreign blood in his veins. On the other hand, those men to whom he spoke, though highly educated, were but superstitious Egyptians who could not relieve themselves of the belief that a divine power rested upon the Pharaoh. Thus his speculative young brain poured its fantasies into attentive minds unbiased by rival speculations, though narrowed by conventions. Egyptians, ever lacking in originality, have always possessed the power to imitate and adapt ; and those nobles whose fortunes were dependent upon the royal favour soon learnt to attune their minds to the note of their king. Daily they must have gone about their business ostentatiously attempting to hold to the difficult path of truth ; laboriously telling themselves what wonders the new thought revealed to them ; loudly praising the wisdom of the boy-Pharaoh ; and nervously asking themselves whether and when the wrath of Amon would smite them.

Thus encouraged, the king and his mother developed their speculations, and drew into their circle of followers some of the greatest nobles of the land. A striking example of this proselytising is to be found in the tomb of the Vizir Ramose. It has already been stated that that official had constructed for himself a sepulchre in the Theban necropolis, upon the walls of which he had first caused a portrait of the young king to be sculptured in the old conventional style, and later had added another portrait of the Pharaoh standing beneath the radiating beams of the sun, executed in the new style. Ramose now added various other scenes and inscriptions, and he records a certain speech made by the king to him, and his own reply.

> " The words of Ra," the king had said, " are before thee. . . . My august father[1] taught me their essence and [revealed] them to me. . . . They were known in my heart, opened to my face. I understood. . . ."
>
> " Thou art the Only One of Aton ; in possession of his designs," replied Ramose. " Thou hast directed the mountains. The fear of thee is in the midst of their secret chambers, as it is in the hearts of the people. The mountains hearken to thee as the people hearken."

Thus one sees how the king was already formulating some kind of doctrine in his head, and that the nobles were receiving it ; but it is significant that there are here representations of Ramose loaded with gifts by the Pharaohs, as though in reward for his allegiance. The Pharaoh seems, indeed, to have showered honours upon those who appeared to grasp intelligently the thoughts which were still immature in his own head ; and there must have been many an antagonist who rallied to his standard from the sheer love of gold. The king was in need of all the support which he could muster, for an open break with the priesthood of Amon-Ra grew more and more probable as his doctrines shaped themselves in

[1] Meaning the god.

his mind; and although the people of Egypt as a whole would, without question, follow their Pharaoh for the one reason that he *was* Pharaoh, there was every probability that the Amon priesthood and the Theban populace would make a stand against any infringement of the rights of their local god.

The young Pharaoh seems to have been very strong-willed, and one may presume that he inherited, from his illustrious fathers, the forceful character which there is not a little evidence to show they possessed. Throughout his life, and for some years after his death, he retained the affection of his people; and when one considers how faithfully his nobles followed him so long as he had strength and health to lead them, and how completely lost they were at his death, one realises how great an influence he must have exerted over them. Even at this early age they seem to have possessed a deep regard for the grave, thoughtful boy; and behind all the pretence, the hypocrisy, and the merely conventional loyalty, one surely catches a glimpse of a strong, personal affection for the king.

We must here record the birth of the king's first daughter, which occurred in about the fifth year of his reign, when he was some eighteen years of age. The child was named Merytaton. "Beloved of Aton"; and though the advent of

a daughter instead of a son must have been a grave disappointment to the royal couple, a remarkable degree of affection was lavished upon the little girl, as will be apparent in the sequel.

9. THE NATURE OF THE NEW RELIGION

There was nothing strikingly exalted in the religion which was now so filling the king's mind. Ra-Horakhti Aton was in no wise considered as the only god: there were as yet no ideas of monotheism in the doctrine. In the new temple at Karnak, as we have seen, Horus, Set, Wepwat, and other gods were named; and elsewhere Amon was reluctantly recognised. The goddess Maat, in the tomb of Ramose, was not obliterated from the walls, but still stood protecting the king; and in the same tomb Horus of Edfu is invoked. In the tomb of Horemheb, Horus, Osiris, Isis, Nephthys, and Hathor are mentioned, and the gods of the Necropolis still receive honour; Horemheb himself still holds the honorary post of High Priest of Horus, Lord of Alabastronpolis; Thoth and Maat are referred to; and there is a magical prayer to Ra, which is by no means of lofty character. Scarabs of this period speak of the Pharaoh as beloved of Thoth, the god of wisdom; and in a letter to the king dated in the fifth year of his reign, Ptah and " the gods and goddesses" of Memphis are referred to.

This letter is of such interest that a fuller account of it must here be given. It was addressed to the king, who is still called Amenophis, by a royal steward named Apiy, who lived at Memphis. Two copies of the letter were found at Gurob,[1] both dated in the fifth year of the king's reign, the third month of winter, and the nineteenth day. The letter begins with the full titles of the Pharaoh, including "Great of Dominion in Karnak," and "Ruler of Thebes," and also the phrase "living in truth," which from this time onwards was always added to his name. Then follows the invocation: "May Ptah of the beautiful countenance work for thee, who created thy beauties, thy true father who raised (?) thee from his house to rule the orbit of the Aton." Next comes the real business of the letter: "A communication is this to the Master, [to whom be] life, prosperity, and health, to give information that the temple of thy father Ptah . . . is sound and prosperous; the house of Pharaoh . . . is flourishing; the establishments of Pharaoh . . . are flourishing; the residence of Pharaoh . . . is flourishing and healthy; the offerings of all the gods and goddesses who are upon the soil (?) of Memphis are . . . complete; complete [are they], there is

---

[1] Griffith: Kahun Papyri. Text, p. 91.

nothing held back from them." Again the titles
of the king are given, and the letter ends with
the date.

Thus in the fifth year of the king's reign, when
he was about eighteen years of age, the various
gods of Egypt were still acknowledged ; and,
though the art had been changed and the worship
of Ra-Horakhti under the name of Aton had
made great strides towards supremacy, there is
as yet no sign of the lofty monotheism which
the Pharaoh was soon to propound.

In the portions of the tomb of Horemheb which
date from this period, Ra-Horakhti is invoked
in the following words : " Ra-Horakhti, great
god, Lord of heaven, Lord of earth, who cometh
forth from his horizon and illuminateth the Two
Lands [of Egypt], the sun of darkness as the
great one, as Ra ; " and again : " Ra, Lord of
Truth, great god, sovereign of Heliopolis, . . .
Horakhti, only god, king of the gods, who rises
in the west and sendeth forth his beauty." From
other sources, which we have seen, the god is
called " Ra-Horakhti rejoicing in the horizon
in his name Heat-which-is-in-Aton."

Here we have simply the old religion of Heliopolis, to which has been grafted something of
the doctrines of the Syrian Adonis or Aton.
At Heliopolis there was a sacred bull, known
as Mnevis, which was regarded as the living

personification of Ra-Horakhti, and which was treated with divine honours, like the more famous Apis bull of Memphis. Even this superstition was accepted by the king at this time, and continued to be acknowledged by him for yet another year or two.[1] The " Heat-which-is-in Aton " offered food for much speculation, and, by directing the attention to an intangible quality of the sun, opened up the widest fields for religious thought. But, with this exception, there was nothing as yet in the new religion to command one's admiration.

[1] Is there a distant connection between Mnevis and the Minoan bull of Crete ? See p. 117.

III

AKHNATON FOUNDS A NEW CITY

*" A brave soul, undauntedly facing the momentum of immemorial tradition . . . that he might disseminate ideas far beyond and above the capacity of his age to understand."—*BREASTED: *" History of Egypt."*

1. THE BREAK WITH THE PRIESTHOOD OF AMON-RA

THE expected break with the priesthood of Amon was not long in coming. One knows nothing of the details of the quarrel, but it may be supposed that Akhnaton himself flung down the gauntlet, making the rash attempt to rid himself of the weight of an organisation which had proved such a drag upon his actions. There is no evidence to show that he disbanded the priesthood, or prohibited the worship of Amon at this period of his reign ; but as the ultimate persecution of that god, some years later, commenced very soon after the death of his mother, one may suppose that it was her restraining influence which prevented him from precipitating

a struggle to the death with the god of Thebes.
The king was now entering upon the sixth year
of his reign and the nineteenth of his age, and
he was already developing in his mind theories
and principles which were soon to produce radical
changes in the new religion of the Court. He
found, no doubt, that it was hopeless to attempt
to convert the people of Thebes to the new
doctrines ; and daily he realised the more clearly
that the development either of the faith of Ra-
Horakhti Aton, or of the ideals which he was
beginning to find therein, was cramped and
checked by the hostility of the influences which
pressed around his immediate circle. From the
walls of every temple, from pylons and gateways,
pillars and obelisks, the figure of Amon stared
down at him in defiance ; and everywhere he
was confronted with the tokens of that god's
power. His little temple at Karnak was over-
shadowed by the larger buildings of Amon ;
and the few priests who served at the new altar
were lost amidst the crowds of the ministers of
the Theban god. How could the flower thrive
and bloom in such uncongenial soil ? How could
the sun shine through such density of conventional tradition ?

The king, no doubt, endeavoured to cripple
the priesthood of Amon by cutting down its
budget as much as possible, and by attempting

to win over to his side some of the priests of
high standing. Had he succeeded in reducing
it to the rank of the smaller cults, it is probable
that he would have been satisfied so to leave it ;
for at that time he wished only to place Ra-
Horakhti in a position of undoubted supremacy
above all other gods. But the vast resources
of Amon seemed unconquerable, and there
appeared to be little chance of reducing the
priesthood to a position of inferior rank.

In this dilemma the king took a step which
had been for some time considered in his mind
and in the minds of his advisers. He decided
to abandon Thebes. He would build a city far
away from all contaminating influences, and there
he would hold his court and worship his god.
On clean, new soil he would establish the earthly
home of Ra-Horakhti Aton, and there, with
his faithful followers, he would develop those
schemes which now so filled his brain. Thus
also, by reducing Thebes to the position of
a provincial town, he might lessen the power of
the priesthood of Amon ; for no longer would
Amon be the royal god, the god of the capital.
He would shake the dust of Thebes from off his
sandals, and never again would he allow himself
to be baffled and irritated by the sight of the
glories of Amon.

The first step which he took was that of

changing his name from Amenophis " The-Peace-
of-Amon," to Akhnaton, " Aton is satisfied " ;[1]
and from that time forth the word Amon hardly
passed his lips. He retained two of his other
names,—*i.e.*, " Beautiful-is-the-being-of-Ra," and
" The-Only-One-of-Ra," the latter being often
used by him ; but such titles and names as that
which made mention of Karnak he entirely dispensed with. He now laid more stress upon the
nature of his god as " Aton " or " the Aton "[2]
than as Ra-Horakhti ; and from this time onwards the name Ra-Horakhti becomes less and
less prominent, though retained throughout the
king's reign.

2. AKHNATON SELECTS THE SITE OF HIS CITY

Down the river it would seem that the young
Pharaoh now sailed in his royal *dahabiyeh*, looking to right and left as he went, now inspecting
this site and now examining that. At last he
came upon a place which suited his fancy to
perfection. It was situated about 160 miles
above the modern Cairo. At this point the limestone cliffs upon the east bank leave the river
and recede for about three miles, returning to

[1] Sethe : Zeitschrift Aeg. Spr., 44, 116-118.

[2] The god is sometimes called " Aton " simply and sometimes
Pa Aton, " the Aton " ; just as we speak of " Christ " or " the Christ,"
and of " Lord " or " the Lord," this latter being the actual meaning
of " Aton."

the water some five or six miles farther along.
Thus a bay is formed which is protected on its
west side by the river in which there here lies
a small island, and in all other directions by the
crescent of the cliffs. Upon the island he would
erect pavilions and pleasure-houses. Along the
edge of the river there was a narrow strip of
cultivated land whereon he would plant his
palace gardens, and those of the nobles' villas.
Behind this verdant band the smooth desert
stretched, and here he would build the palace
itself and the great temples. Behind this again,
the sand and gravel surface of the wilderness
gently sloped up to the foot of the cliffs, and here
there would be roads and causeways whereon
the chariots might be whirled in the early
mornings. In the face of the cliffs he would cut
his tomb and those of his followers ; and at
intervals around the crescent of these hills he
would cause great boundary stones to be made,
so that all men might know and respect the
limits of his city. What splendid quays would
edge the river, what palaces reflect their white-
ness in its waters ! There would be broad shaded
avenues, and shimmering lakes surrounded by
the fairest trees of Asia. Temples would raise
their lofty pylons to the blue skies, and broad
courts should lie stretched in the sunlight.

In Akhnaton's youthful mind there already

H

stood the temples and the mansions; already he heard the sound of sweet music. The pomp of imperial Egypt displaced the farm-houses and the fields of corn which now occupied the site; and the song of the shepherd in the wilderness was changed to the rolling psalms of the Aton. Fair was this dream and enthralling to the dreamer. To Queen Tiy it probably did not appeal so strongly; for Thebes was full of associations to her, and her palace beside the lake was very dear. There is, indeed, every reason to suppose that the dowager-queen lived on at Thebes after her son had abandoned it.

3. THE FIRST FOUNDATION INSCRIPTION

Preparations were soon made for the laying out of the city, and in a very short time Akhnaton was called upon to visit the site in order to perform the foundation ceremonies. Fortunately the inscriptions upon some of the boundary tablets in the desert tell us something of the manner in which the king marked the limits of the city.[1] The first inscription reads as follows :—

> Year 6, fourth month of the second season, day 13.[2] . . . On this day the King was in the

---

[1] The translation here given is based upon that published by Davies in Amarna V.; but the year cannot be the fourth, as there stated as probable, since in the above-mentioned letter dated in year 5 the king is still called Amenophis, whereas in this inscription he is called Akhnaton.

[2] The day is not certain; perhaps it is day 4.

City of the Horizon of Aton.[1] His Majesty ascended a great chariot of electrum, [appearing] like Aton when He rises from His [eastern] horizon and fills the land with His love ; and he started a goodly course [from his camping place] to the City of the Horizon. . . . Heaven was joyful, earth was glad, and every heart was happy when they saw him. And his Majesty offered a great sacrifice to Aton, of bread, beer, horned bulls, polled bulls, beasts, fowl, wine, incense, frankincense, and all goodly herbs on this day of demarcating the city of the Horizon. . . .

After these things, the good pleasure of Aton being done, . . . [the King returned from] the City of the Horizon, and he rested upon his great throne with which he is well pleased, which uplifts his beauties. And his Majesty continued in the presence of his Father Aton, and Aton shone upon him in life and length of days, invigorating his body each day.

And his Majesty said, " Bring me the companions of the King, the great ones and the mighty ones, the captains of soldiers, and the nobles of the land in its entirety." And they were conducted to him straightway, and they lay on their bellies before his Majesty, kissing the ground before his mighty will.

And his Majesty said unto them, " Ye behold the City of the Horizon of Aton, which the Aton has desired me to make for Him as a monument in the great name of my Majesty for ever. For it was the Aton, my Father, that brought me to this City of the Horizon. There was not a noble who directed me to it ; there was not any man in the whole land who led me to it, saying, ' It is fitting for his Majesty that he make a City of the Horizon of Aton in this place.' Nay, but it was the Aton, my Father, that

---

[1] For the sake of brevity it is often called " the City of the Horizon," simply, in this volume.

directed me to it to make it for Him. . . . Behold
the Pharaoh found that [this site] belonged not to a
god, nor to a goddess, it belonged not to a prince, nor
to a princess. There was no right for any man to
act as owner of it." . . .

[. . . And they answered and said] " Lo!
it is Aton that putteth [the thought] in thy heart
regarding any place that he desires. He doth not
uplift the name of any King except thy Majesty;
He doth not [exalt] any other except [thee.] . . .

Thou drawest unto Aton every land, thou adornest
for Him the towns which He had made for his own
self, all lands, all countries, the Hanebu[1] with their
products and their tribute upon their backs for Him that
made their life, and by whose rays one lives and
breathes the air. May He grant eternity in seeing
his rays. . . . Verily, the City of the Horizon will
thrive like Aton in heaven for ever and ever."

Then his Majesty lifted his hand to heaven unto
Him that formed him, saying, " As my father Ra-
Horakhti Aton liveth, the great and living Aton,
ordaining life, vigorous in life, my father, my rampart
of a million cubits, my remembrancer of eternity, my
witness of that which pertains to eternity, who formeth
Himself with His own hands, whom no artificer hath
known, who is established in rising and in setting
each day without ceasing. Whether He is in heaven
or in earth,[2] every eye seeth Him without [failing,]
while He fills the land with His beams and makes
every face to live. With seeing whom may my eyes
be satisfied daily, when He rises in this temple of
Aton in the City of the Horizon, and fills it with His
own self by His beams, beauteous in love, and lays

---

[1] Mediterranean people.

[2] This has reference to the rays which come from the Aton.

them upon me in life and length of days for ever and ever.

"I will make the City of the Horizon of Aton for the Aton, my father, in this place. I will not make the City south of it, north of it, west of it, or east of it. I will not pass beyond the southern boundary-stone southward, neither will I pass beyond the northern boundary-stone northward to make for him a City of the Horizon there; neither will I make for Him a city on the western side. Nay, but I will make the City of the Horizon for the Aton, my Father, upon the east side, the place which He did enclose for His own self with cliffs, and made a plain (?) in the midst of it that I might sacrifice to Him thereon: this is it. Neither shall the Queen say unto me, 'Behold, there is a goodly place for the City of the Horizon in another place,' and I hearken unto her. Neither shall any noble nor [any one] of all men who are in the whole land [say unto me], 'Behold, there is a goodly place for the City of the Horizon in another place,' and I hearken unto them. Whether it be down-stream, or southwards, or westwards, or east-wards, I will not say 'I will abandon this City of the Horizon and will hasten away and make the City of the Horizon in this other goodly place' for ever. Nay, but I did find this City of the Horizon for the Aton, which He had himself desired, and with which He is pleased for ever and ever.

"I will make a temple of Aton for the Aton, my Father, in this place. I will make a . . . of Aton for the Aton, my Father, in this place. I will make a Shadow-of-the-Sun[1] of the Great Wife of the King, Nefertiti, for the Aton, my Father, in this place. I will make a House of Rejoicing for the Aton, my Father, on the island of 'Aton illustrious in Festivals'

---

[1] This seems to have been a temple.

in this place. . . . I will make all works which are
necessary for the Aton, my Father, in this place. I
will make . . . for the Aton, my Father, in this place.
I will make for myself the Palace of Pharaoh ; and
I will make the Palace of the Queen in this place.
There shall be made for me a sepulchre in the eastern
hills ; my burial shall be made therein . . . and the
burial of the Great Wife of the King, Nefertiti, shall
be made therein, and the burial of the King's daughter
Merytaton shall be made therein. If I die in any
town of the north, south, west, or east, I will be
brought here and my burial shall be made in the
City of the Horizon. If the Great Queen, Nefertiti,
who lives, die in any town of the north, south, west
or east, she shall be brought here and buried in the
City of the Horizon. If the King's daughter Merytaton
die in any town of the north, south, west, or east,
she shall be brought here and buried in the City of
the Horizon. And the sepulchre of Mnevis shall
be made in the eastern hills and he shall be buried
therein. The tombs of the High Priests and the
Divine Fathers and the priests of the Aton shall
be made in the eastern hills, and they shall be buried
therein. The tombs of the officers, and others, shall
be made in the eastern hills, and they shall be buried
therein.

" For as my father Ra-Horakhti Aton liveth . . .
[the words ?] of the priests, more evil are they than
those things which I heard until the year four, more
evil are they than those things which I have heard
in . . . more evil are they than those things which
King [Nebmaara[1]] heard, more evil are they than
those things which Menkheperura[2] heard. . . . "

---

[1] The second name of Amenophis III., Akhnaton's father.
[2] The second name of Thutmosis IV., Akhnaton's grandfather.

The rest of the inscription is so much broken that only a few words here and there can be read. They seem to refer to the king's further projects—how he will make ships to sail to and from the city, how he will build granaries, celebrate festivals, plant trees, and so on.

The reference to the year four is very interesting, and it would seem that it was at about that date that the king's eyes were opened to the necessity of making war upon the priesthood of Amon. As we have seen, it was in about the fourth year of his reign that the great changes in the art took place, and the symbol of the sun's rays was introduced into the sculptures. The mention of the two previous Pharaohs shows that troubles were already brewing then ; but it had remained for the energetic young Akhnaton to bring matters to a head.

4. THE SECOND FOUNDATION INSCRIPTION

The inscription recording these events was probably not written until some months after they had occurred. Just when the engravers had made an end of their work a second daughter was born to the king and queen, whom they named Meketaton ; and orders were given that her figure should be added upon the boundary tablet beside that of her sister, which already appeared there with Akhnaton and Nefertiti.

The king must have been greatly distressed that
a son had not been granted to him ; for the
thought was bitter that, in the event of his death,
all his projects would fall to the ground. He
therefore altered the wording of the inscriptions
about to be written on the other boundary
tablets ; and, by including his oath in the text,
he added an even greater integrity to the
decree. The name of the second daughter was
now inserted in this inscription, which reads :—

> Year six, fourth month of the second season,
> thirteenth day.
>
> On this day the King was in the City of the
> Horizon of Aton, in the parti-coloured tent made
> for his Majesty in the City of the Horizon, the name
> of which is "The Aton is well pleased." And his
> Majesty ascended a great chariot of electrum, drawn
> by a span of horses, and [he appeared] like Aton
> when He rises from the horizon and fills the two lands
> with His love. And he started a goodly course to the
> City of the Horizon, on this the first occasion,
> . . . to dedicate it as a monument to the Aton,
> even as his father Ra-Horakhti Aton had given
> command. . . . And he caused a great sacrifice
> to be offered.
>
> And his Majesty went southward, and halted on
> his chariot before his father Ra-Horakhti Aton, at
> the [foot of the] south-east hills, and Aton shone upon
> him in life and length of days, invigorating his body
> every day.
>
> Now this is the oath pronounced by the King :—
>
> "As my Father Ra-Horakhti Aton liveth, as my
> heart is happy in the Queen and her children—as to
> whom may it be granted that the Great Wife of the

King, Nefertiti, living for ever and ever, grow aged
after a multitude of years, in the care of the Pharaoh,
and may it be granted that the King's daughter
Merytaton and the King's daughter Meketaton, her
children, grow old in the care of the Great Wife of
the King, their mother. . . .

" This is my oath of truth which it is my desire
to pronounce, and of which I will not say ' It is false'
eternally for ever.

" The southern boundary-stone which is on the
eastern hills. It is the boundary-stone of the City
of the Horizon, namely this one by which I have made
halt. I will not pass beyond it southwards for ever
and ever. Make the south-west boundary-stone
opposite it on the western hills of the City of the
Horizon exactly.

" The middle boundary-stone which is on the
eastern hills. It is the boundary-stone of the City
of the Horizon by which I have made halt on the
eastern hills of the City of the Horizon. I will not
pass beyond it eastwards for ever and ever. Make
the middle boundary-stone which is to be on the
western hills opposite it exactly.

" The north-eastern boundary-stone by which I
have made halt. It is the northern boundary-stone
of the City of the Horizon. I will not pass beyond
it down-stream for ever and ever. Make the north
boundary-stone which is to be on the western hills
opposite it exactly.

" And the City of the Horizon of Aton extends
from the south boundary-stone as far as the north
boundary-stone, measured between boundary-stone
and boundary-stone on the eastern hills [which
measurement] amounts to 6 *ater*,[1] ¾ *khe*, and 4

---

[1] The *ater* corresponds to the Greek *schoinos*, and the *khe* is the
schoenium of 100 cubits, 40 *khe* making one *ater*.

cubits. Likewise from the south-west boundary-
stone to the north-west boundary-stone on the
western hills [the measurement] amounts to 6 *ater*,
¾ *khe*, and 4 cubits likewise exactly.

"And the area within these four boundary-stones
from the eastern hills to the western hills is the City
of the Horizon of Aton in its proper self. It belongs
to my Father Ra-Horakhti Aton: mountains, deserts,
meadows, islands, high-ground, low-ground, land,
water, villages, embankments, men, beasts, groves,
and all things which the Aton my Father shall bring
into existence for ever and ever.

"I will not neglect this oath which I have made
to the Aton my Father for ever and ever; nay, but
it shall be set on a tablet of stone as the south-east
boundary, likewise as the north-east boundary of
the City of the Horizon; and it shall be set likewise
on a tablet of stone as the south-west boundary,
likewise as the north-west boundary of the City of
the Horizon. It shall not be erased, it shall not be
washed out, it shall not be kicked, it shall not be
struck with stones, its spoiling shall not be brought
about. If it be missing, if it be spoilt, if the tablet
on which it is shall fall, I will renew it again afresh
in the place in which it was."

5. THE DEPARTURE FROM THEBES

From the above inscription one sees that
Akhnaton had now decided to include the west
bank of the river, opposite to the original site,
in the new domain; and the great boundary
tablets are there to be found as on the eastern
side. By the time these decrees were engraved
the Pharaoh was nearly eighteen years of age;

and these developments in his plans are the natural signs of the progress of his brain towards that of a grown man.

Having laid the foundations of the city, the king probably returned to Thebes, where he waited as patiently as possible for his dream to take concrete form. This period of waiting must have been peculiarly trying to him, for his troubles with the Amon priesthood must have embittered his days. He seems, however, to have been extremely devoted to his wife, Nefertiti, who was now, it would seem, a curiously attractive young woman of fifteen or sixteen years of age ;[1] and the arrival of the second baby afforded an interest which meant much to him. One may now picture the king and queen living, in the seclusion of the palace, a homely, simple existence, ever dwelling in a happy day-dream upon the future glories of the new city, and the rising power of the religion of Aton. Akhnaton's ill-health, of course, must have caused both his friends and himself much anxiety ; but even this had its compensations, for those who suffer from epilepsy are by the gods beloved, and Akhnaton, no doubt, believed the hallucinations due to his disease to be god-given visions. There must have been a very considerable amount

[1] The unpublished head in Berlin is that of a strange, dreamy, heavy-eyed girl.

of business to be worked through in connection with the building of the city, and he could have had little time to brood upon what he now considered to be the wrongs inflicted upon him and his house by the priests of Amon.

So passed the seventh year of his reign without any particular records to mark it. At Aswan there is a monument which perhaps dates from about this period. The king's chief sculptor, Bek, was there employed in obtaining red granite for the decoration of the new city; and he caused to be made upon a large rock a commemorative tablet. On it one sees him before Akhnaton, whose figure has been erased at a later date; and the altar of the Aton, above which are the usual sun's rays, stands beside them. Bek calls himself " The Chief of the Works in the Red [Granite] Hills, the assistant whom his Majesty himself taught, Chief of the Sculptors on the great and mighty monuments of the king in the house of Aton in the City of the Horizon of Aton." Here also one sees Men, the father of Bek, who was also Chief of the Sculptors, presenting an offering to a statue of Amenophis III, under whom he had served.

The eighth year of Akhnaton's reign, and the twenty-first year of his age, was memorable, for it would seem that he now took up his permanent residence in the City of the Horizon. On some of the boundary tablets a repetition of the royal oath is recorded ; and, as this is the last mention of a *visit* made by Akhnaton to the new capital, one may suppose that henceforth he was resident there. The inscription reads :—

> This oath (of the sixth year) was repeated in year eight, first month of the second season, eighth day. The King was in the City of the Horizon of Aton, and Pharaoh stood mounted on a great chariot of electrum, inspecting the boundary-stones of the Aton. . . .

Then follows a list of these boundary-stones, and the inscription ends with the words :—

> And the breadth of the City of the Horizon of Aton is from cliff to cliff, from the eastern horizon of heaven to the western horizon of heaven. It shall be for my Father Ra-Horakhti Aton, its hills, its deserts, all its fowl, all its people, all its cattle, all things which the Aton produces, on which His rays shine, all things which are in . . . the City of the Horizon, they shall be for the Father, the living Aton, unto the temple of Aton in the City of the Horizon for ever and ever ; they are all offered to His spirit. And may His rays be beauteous when they receive them.

Thus was the king's city planned and laid out. The two years of feverish work had probably produced considerable results, and already we may picture the city taking form. The royal palace was perhaps almost finished by now, and the villas of some of the nobles were habitable. With many a sigh of relief Akhnaton must have

bade farewell to Thebes. A third daughter,
who was named Ankhsenpaaton, had just been
born ; and one may thus picture the royal party
which sailed down the river as being very distinctly a family. One sees Akhnaton, a sickly
young man of twenty-one years of age, walking
to and fro upon the deck of the royal vessel,
with his hand upon the shoulder of his young
wife, in whose arms the baby princess is carried.
Beside them are the other two princesses, one
somewhat over two years of age, the other
about four years. The queen's sister, Nezemmut,
records of whose existence soon become apparent,
was perhaps also of the party. Ay and Ty,
the father and step-mother of Nefertiti, were
doubtless with the royal family now as they
sailed down the river ; and several of the nobles
who play a part in the following pages no doubt
formed the suite which attended to the royal
commands.

6. THE AGE OF AKHNATON

We have spoken of the king as being twenty-
one years old. The story has now reached
a point at which we must pause to consider this
vexed question of Akhnaton's age. In the above
pages it has been said that the Pharaoh was
about thirteen years old at his marriage and
accession to the throne ; was sixteen or seventeen

when the canons of art were changed and the symbols of the Aton religion introduced ; was nineteen when the foundations of the new city were laid ; and was twenty-one when he took up his residence there. Let us study these ages in the above order.

Firstly, then, as to the king's marriage. The mummy of Thutmosis IV, the grandfather of Akhnaton, has been shown by Professor Elliot Smith to be that of a man not more than about twenty-six years of age. That king was succeeded by his son Amenophis III, who is known to have been married to Queen Tiy before the second year of his reign, and to have been old enough at that time to begin to hunt big game. It would be difficult to believe that he would be permitted to join any hunting party, however secure against accident, before the twelfth year of his age ; but, on the other hand, if he were more than that age, his father would have to have been less than twelve at *his* marriage. Thus the only possible conclusion is that both Thutmosis IV and Amenophis III were barely thirteen when they were married, and very possibly even younger. This is shown to be a correct conclusion by the fact that the mummy of Amenophis III has been pronounced by Professor Elliot Smith to be that of a man of forty-five or fifty ; and as he reigned thirty-six years he must have been *at most* fourteen, and probably some years younger, at his accession and marriage.

There is not sufficient evidence to show at what ages the previous Pharaohs of the dynasty had married, but as Akhnaton's father and grandfather entered into matrimony at this early age, it would not be safe to suppose that he himself delayed his marriage till a later age. Queen Tiy was in all probability married when she was ten or eleven years old.[1] Akhnaton's daughter Merytaton, who was born in the fourth or fifth year of his reign, was, as will be seen in due course, married before the seventeenth year of the reign—that is to say, when she was twelve or younger. The Princess Ankhsenpaaton, who was born in the eighth year, was married, at latest, two years after Akhnaton's death— *i.e.*, when she was eleven. Another of Akhnaton's daughters, Neferneferuaton, who has not yet appeared, was born in her father's eleventh year, and was married before the fifteenth, and there- fore could only have been four or five years of age.

Child-marriages such as these are common in Egypt, even at the present day. Those who have lived on the Nile, and have studied the national habits, will assuredly fix the probable age of a royal *mariage de convenance* at about thirteen years.

---

[1] See note on p. 154.

Secondly, as to Akhnaton's age at the changing of the art. In the biography of Bakenkhonsu, the High Priest of Amon under Rameses II, that official tells us that he arrived at the state of manhood at the age of sixteen, and one may therefore suppose that this was the recognised legal age at which a man became a responsible agent in Egypt. Now it has been clearly seen that Akhnaton was under the regency of his mother during the first years of his reign, and mention has been made of the inscription at Wady Hammamat, where, although the new symbol of the religion is shown, Queen Tiy's name is placed beside that of her son in an equally honourable position. She was thus still Queen Regent when the art was changed, and her son could not yet have come of age—*i.e.*, he must then have been under sixteen.

Thirdly, we have to consider the question of his age when he laid the foundations of the new city. This was the first decisive action performed by the king in which his mother has no concern, and of which she perhaps even disapproved, and it surely marks the period at which he took the government into his own hands. If, like Bakenkhonsu, he came of age at sixteen, in the fourth year of his reign, the founding of the new capital in the sixth year would well fit in with the supposition that the first idea of abandoning

I

Thebes marks the date of the king's arrival at
maturity. It will be recalled that on the
foundation stela he speaks of the year four as
marking a definite epoch.

It may be asked how so young a person could
conceive that great dream of the new city dedicated to the Aton. But, after all, he was
nineteen years of age when he had properly
developed the plan, and twenty-one when he
took up his residence there. Akhnaton's great-
ness, as will be seen later, dates from the height
of his reign in the City of the Horizon, and not
from his early years. Still, when one calls to
mind the infant prodigies, the child preachers
who stir an audience at an early age, one may
credit a boy of eighteen or nineteen with the
planning of a new city. Even in the cold Occi-
dent such youthful thinkers are not rare, and
surely they blossom forth less infrequently in
the maturing warmth of the Orient. The Caliph
El Hakkîm, for instance, came to the throne
at eleven and was only sixteen when he issued
his first religious and political decrees.

IV

AKHNATON FORMULATES THE
RELIGION OF ATON

———

" No such grand theology had ever appeared in the world before, so far as we know ; and it is the forerunner of the later monotheist religions."—PETRIE : " The Religion of Ancient Egypt."

" Akhnaton was a God-intoxicated man, whose mind responded with marvellous sensitiveness and discernment to the visible evidences of God about him."—BREASTED : "Religion and Thought in Ancient Egypt."

———

1. ATON THE TRUE GOD

AMIDST the fair palaces and verdant gardens of the new city, Akhnaton, now a man of some twenty-two years, turned his thoughts fully to the development of his religion. It is necessary, therefore, for us to glance at the essential features of this the most enlightened doctrine of the ancient world, and in some degree to make ourselves acquainted with the creed which the king himself was evolving out of that worship of Ra-Horakhti Aton in which he had been educated.

Originally the Aton was the actual sun's disk ;

but, as has been said, the god was now called
" Heat-which-is-in-Aton," and Akhnaton, con-
centrating his attention on this aspect of the
godhead, drew the eyes of his followers toward
a force far more intangible and distant than
the dazzling orb to which they bowed down.
Akhnaton's conception of God, as we now begin
to observe it, was as the power which created
the sun, the energy which penetrated to this
earth in the sun's heat and caused all things
to grow. At the present day the scientist will
tell you that God is the ultimate source of life,
that where natural explanation fails there God
is to be found : He is, in a word, the author
of energy, the primal motive-power of all known
things. Akhnaton, centuries upon centuries before the birth of the scientist, defined God in
just this manner. In an age when men believed,
as some do still, that a deity was but an
exaggerated creature of this earth, having a form
built on material lines, this youthful Pharaoh
proclaimed God to be the formless essence, the
intelligent germ, the loving force, which perme-
ated time and space. Let it be clearly understood
that the Aton as conceived by the young Pharaoh
was in no sense one of those old deities which
our God ultimately replaced in Egypt. The
Aton is God almost as we conceive Him. There
is no quality attributed by the king to the Aton

which we do not attribute to our God. Like
a flash of blinding light in the night-time the
Aton stands out for a moment amidst the black
Egyptian darkness, and disappears once more—
the first signal to this world of the future religion
of the West.   No man whose mind is free from
prejudice will fail to see a far closer resemblance
to the teachings of Christ in the religion of
Akhnaton than in that of Abraham, Isaac, and
Jacob.   The faith of the patriarchs is the lineal
ancestor of the Christian faith ; but the creed
of Akhnaton is its isolated prototype.   One
might believe that Almighty God had for a
moment revealed himself to Egypt, and had
been more clearly, though more momentarily,
interpreted there than ever He was in Syria or
Palestine before the time of Christ.

2. ATON THE TENDER FATHER OF ALL CREATION

Amon-Ra and the old gods of Egypt were,
for the most part, but deified mortals, endued
with monstrous, though limited, powers, and
still having around them traditions of aggrandised
human deeds.   Others, we have seen, had their
origin in natural phenomena ; the wind, the Nile,
the starry heavens, and the like.   All were
terrific or revengeful, if so they had a mind to
be, and all were able to be removed by human

emotions.   But to Akhnaton, although he had
absolutely no precedent upon which to launch
his thoughts, God was the intangible and yet
ever-present Father of mankind, made manifest
in sunshine.   The youthful high priest called
upon his subjects to search for their God not
in the confusion of battle nor behind the smoke
of human sacrifices, but amidst the flowers and
the trees, amidst the wild duck and the fishes.
He preached an enlightened nature-study :   in
some respects he was, perhaps, the first apostle
of the Simple Life.

He strove to break down conventional thought,
and ceaselessly he urged his people to worship
" in truth," simply, without an excess of ceremonial.   While the elder gods had been apparent
in natural convulsions and in the more awful
incidents of life, Akhnaton's kindly Father could
be seen in the little details of existence, in the
growing poppies, in the soft wind which filled
the sails of the ships, in the fish which leapt from
the river.   Like a greater than he, Akhnaton
taught his disciples to address their maker as
their " Father which art in Heaven."   The Aton
was the joy which caused the young sheep " to
dance upon their legs," and the birds " to flutter
in their marshes."   He was the god of the simple
pleasures of life ;   and although Akhnaton himself
was indeed a man of sorrows, plenteously

acquainted with grief, happiness was the watch-word which he gave to his followers.

Akhnaton did not permit any graven image to be made of the Aton. The True God, said the king, had no form; and he held to this opinion throughout his life. The symbol of the religion was the sun's disk, from which there extended numerous rays, each ray ending in a hand; but this symbol was not worshipped. To Christians, in the same way, the cross is the symbol of their creed; but the cross itself is not worshipped. Never before had man conceived a formless deity, a god who was not endowed with the five human senses. The Hebrew patriarchs believed God to be capable of walking in a garden in the cool of the evening, to have made man in His own image, to be possessed of face, form, and hinder parts. But Akhnaton, stemming with his hand the flood of tradition, boldly proclaimed God to be a life-giving, intangible essence : the *heat* which is in the sun. He was " the living Aton"—that is to say, the power which produced and sustained the energy and movement of the sun. Although he was so often called " the Aton," he was more closely defined as " the Master of the Aton."[1] The flaming glory of the sun was the most practical symbol of the godhead, and the warm rays of sunshine constituted the most

[1] Davies, Amarna, I. 45.

obvious connection between heaven and earth ; but always Akhnaton attempted to raise the eyes of the thinkers beyond this visible or understandable expression of divinity, to strain them upwards in the effort to discern that which was " behind the veil." In lighting on a motive power more remote than the sun, and acting through the sun, the young Pharaoh may be said to have penetrated as far behind the eternal barrier as one may ever hope to penetrate this side the churchyard. But though so remote, the Aton was the tender, loving Father of all men, ever-present and ever-mindful of his creatures. There dropped not a sigh from the lips of a babe that the intangible Aton did not hear ; no lamb bleated for its mother but the remote Aton hastened to soothe it. He was the loving " Father and Mother of all that He had made," who " brought up millions by His bounty."

The destructive qualities of the sun were never referred to, and that pitiless orb under which Egypt sweats and groans for the summer months each year had nothing in common with the gentle Father conceived by Akhnaton. The Aton was " the Lord of Love." He was the tender nurse who " creates the man-child in woman, and soothes him that he may not weep " ; whose love, to use an Egyptian phrase of exquisite tenderness, " makes the hands to faint." His beams were " beauteous with love " as they fell upon His people and upon His city, " very rich in love." " Thy love is great and large," says one of Akhnaton's psalms. " Thou fillest the two lands of Egypt with Thy love ; " and another passage runs : " Thy rays encompass the lands. . . . Thou bindest them with Thy love."

Surely never in the history of the world had man conceived a god who " so loved the world." One may search the inscriptions in vain for any reference to a malignant power, to vengeance, to jealousy, or to hatred. The Hebrew psalmist said of God, " Like as a father pitieth his children, even so is the Lord merciful " ; and Akhnaton, many a century before those words were written, attributed just such a nature to the Aton. The Aton was compassionate, was merciful, was gentle, was tender ; He knew not anger, and there was no wrath in Him. His overflowing love reached down the paths of life from mankind to the beasts of the field and to the little flowers themselves. " All flowers blow," says one of Akhnaton's hymns, " and that which grows on the soil thrives at Thy dawning, O Aton. They drink their fill [of warmth] before Thy face. All cattle leap upon their feet ; the birds that were in the nest fly forth with joy ; their wings which were closed move quickly with praise to the living Aton."

One stands amazed as one reads in pompous
Egypt of a god who listens " when the chicken
crieth in the egg-shell," and gives him life,
delighting that he should " chirp with all his
might " when he is hatched forth ; who finds
pleasure in causing " the birds to flutter in their
marshes, and the sheep to dance upon their feet."
For the first time in the history of man the real
meaning of God, as we now understand it, had
been comprehended ; and the idea of a beneficent
Creator who, though remote, spiritual, and
impersonal, could love each one of His creatures,
great or small, had been grasped by this young
Pharaoh. God's unspeakable goodness and
loving-kindness were as clearly interpreted by
Akhnaton as ever they have been by mortal
man ; and the wonder of it lies in this, that
Akhnaton had absolutely nothing to base his
theories upon. He was, so far as we know, the
first man to whom God revealed Himself as the
passionless, all-loving essence of unqualified
goodness.

3. ATON WORSHIPPED AT SUNRISE AND SUNSET.

In order to prevent the more ignorant of his
disciples from worshipping the sun itself Akhnaton
seems to have selected the sunrise and the sunset
as the two hours for ceremonial adoration ; for
then the light, the beauty, the tenderness, of

the celestial phenomenon could be appreciated, and the awful majesty of the sun was not in great prominence. Akhnaton attempted to cultivate in his followers an appreciation of the gentle hues of daybreak and of evening ; and he taught them to believe that the oft-mentioned " beauties" of the Aton were only to be fully understood at these times. In the gladness of sunrise and in the hush of the sunset, the emotions are most apt to be touched and moved ; for in Egypt there is always praise in the heart in the cool opalescence of the dawn, and in the red dusk there is many and many a dream.

Phrases such as the following may be gleaned from Akhnaton's hymns : " Thy rising is beautiful in the horizon of heaven, O living Aton, who dispensest life ; shining from the eastern horizon of heaven, Thou fillest Egypt with Thy beauty." " Thy setting is beautiful, O living Aton, . . . who guidest . . . all countries that they may make laudations at Thy dawning and at Thy setting." " When the Aton rises all the land is in joy ; His rays produce eyes for all that He has created ; and men say, ' It is life to see Him, there is death in not seeing Him.' " " When Thou settest alive,[1] O Aton, West and East give praise to Thee." " Thou settest behind the western horizon ; Thou settest in life and gladness,

---

[1] The idea is that the Aton does not die as dies the sunlight.

and every eye rejoices though they are in darkness after Thou settest." "When Thou hast risen they live ; when Thou settest they die."

The ceremonial side of the religion does not seem to have been complex. The priests, of whom there were very few, offered sacrifices, consisting mostly of vegetables, fruit, and flowers, to the Aton, and at these ceremonies the king and his family often officiated. They then sang psalms and offered prayers, and, with much sweet music, gave praise to the great Father of joy and love. The Aton, however, was not thought to delight in these ceremonies as He did in more natural thanksgivings. Why should God be praised in set phrases and studied poses when all the fair world was shouting for the joy of Him ? The young calf frisking through the poppy-covered meadows, the birds singing upon the trees, the clouds racing across the sky, were the true worshippers of God.

One of the recently discovered sayings of Christ closely parallels Akhnaton's utterances. " Ye ask," it runs, " who are those that draw us to the kingdom if the kingdom is in heaven ? The fowls of the air, and all the beasts that are under the earth or upon the earth, and the fishes in the sea, these are they which draw you, and the kingdom is within you." The contemplation of nature was more to Akhnaton than many ceremonies, and his thoughts were more easily drawn upwards by the rustle of the leaves than by the shaking of the systrum.

4. THE GOODNESS OF ATON

In the gardens of the City of the Horizon Akhnaton was surrounded on all sides by the joyous beauties of nature. Here the birds sang merrily in the laden trees, here the cool north wind rustled through the leaves, setting them dancing upon their stems, here the many-coloured blossoms nodded to their reflections in the still lakes; and, as he watched the sunlight playing with the blue shadows, his heart seemed to fill to repletion with gratitude to God. " O Lord, how manifold are Thy works ! " was his constant cry. " The whole land is in joy and holiday because of Thee. They shout to the height of heaven, they receive joy and gladness when they see Thee." How " fair of form " was the formless Aton, how " radiant of colour " ! " All that Thou hast made," said the king, " leaps before Thee." " Thou makest the beauty of form through Thyself alone." " Eyes have life at sight of Thy beauty ; hearts have health when the Aton shines."

As the psalmist sang, " The Lord is my shepherd, I shall not want," so Akhnaton, in the fulness of his heart, cried, " There is no poverty

for him who hath set Thee in his heart; such
an one cannot say, ' O, that I had.' " " When
Thou bringest life to men's hearts by Thy beauty,
there is indeed life." The Aton " gave health
to the eyes by His rays," and, " bright, great,
gleaming, high above all the earth," He was
" the cause of plenty," the very " food and
fatness of Egypt." To David, several centuries
later, God seemed to be " a strong tower of
defence " ; and, thinking along the same lines,
Akhnaton called the Aton his " wall of brass of
a million cubits." The Aton was " the witness
of that which pertains to eternity," and to those
whose thoughts had strayed he was " the remembrancer of eternity." He was the " Lord of
Fate," the " Lord of Fortune," the " Master of
that which is ordained," the " Origin of Fate,"
the " Chance which gives Life " ; and in so
describing him Akhnaton reached a philosophical
position which even to-day is quite unassailable.

Unlike Jehovah, who was described as " great
above all other gods," the Aton was conceived
as being without rivals; and Akhnaton now
never mentions the word " gods." " The living
Aton beside whom there is no other," is one
of the common phrases; and of Him again it is
written, " Thou art alone, but infinite vitalities
are in Thee by means of which to give life to
Thy creatures."

Unlike Jehovah again, who was not infrequently thought to be a wrathful god, surrounded by clouds and darkness, and speaking through the roar of the thunders, the Aton was the "Lord of Peace," who could not tolerate battle and strife. Akhnaton was so opposed to war that he persistently refused to offer an armed resistance to the subsequent revolts which occurred in his Asiatic dominions. The Aton was a deity to whose tender heart human bloodshed made no appeal. In an age of martial glory, when the sword and buckler, the plumed helmet and the shirt of mail, glittered in every street and upon every highway, Akhnaton set himself in opposition to all heroics, and saw God without melodrama.

Above all things the Aton loved truth. Frankness, sincerity, straightforwardness, honesty, and veracity were qualities not always to be found in the heart of an Egyptian ; and Akhnaton, in antagonism to the sins of hypocrisy and deception which he saw around him, always spoke of himself as "living in truth." "I have set truth in my inward parts," says one of his followers, "and falsehood is my loathing ; for I know that the King rejoiceth in truth."

Another point in Akhnaton's teaching is apparent from the scenes, discovered by the present writer, in the tomb of Ramose. There is a scene

often represented upon the walls of tombs of
Dynasty XVIII which seems to represent human
sacrifice.   The figure of a man is seen dragged
to the tomb upon a sledge, and Sir Gaston Maspero
has pointed out that this can hardly be anything
else than such a sacrifice.   This scene was shown
on one of the walls of the tomb of Ramose, and
evidently dated from a period previous to
Akhnaton's revolution.   When, however, the
young king had formulated his religion of love
he could not tolerate a barbaric and cruel ceremony of this kind.   We thus find that the entire
scene is here obliterated, almost certainly by the
king's agents.   The objection to human sacrifice
is closely in accord with his objection to human
suffering as recorded on page 152.

5. AKHNATON THE "SON OF GOD" BY TRADITIONAL RIGHT

It may be understood how the young man
longed for truth in all things when one remembers
the thousand exaggerated conventions of Egyptian
life at this time.   Court etiquette had developed
to a degree which rendered life to the Pharaoh
an endless round of unnatural poses of mind and
body.   In the preaching of his doctrine of truth
and simplicity Akhnaton did not fail to call upon
his subjects to regard their Pharaoh not as a
celestial god, as had been the custom, but as

a man, though, of course, one of divine origin. It was usual for the Pharaoh to keep aloof from his people: Akhnaton was to be found in their midst. The court demanded that their lord should drive in solitary state through the city: Akhnaton stood in his chariot with his wife and

AKHNATON DRIVING WITH HIS WIFE AND DAUGHTER.

children, and allowed the artist to represent him joking therein with his little daughter. In portraying the Pharaoh the artist was expected to draw him in some conventional attitude of dignity: Akhnaton insisted upon being shown in all manner of natural attitudes—now leaning languidly upon a staff, now nursing his children,

K

and now eating his dinner. Thus again one sees his objection to heroics, and his love of naturalness.

But while he strove for truth and sincerity in this manner he did not attempt to remove from his mind the belief in which he had been brought up, that as Pharaoh of Egypt he was himself partly divine. Not only was he by reason of his religion the representative, and hence, in a manner of speech, the " son " of God, but by right of royal descent he was the " son of the Sun." The names of the Pharaohs were always surrounded by an oval band, known as a cartouche, which was the distinguishing mark of a royal name. Akhnaton wrote the name of the Aton within such an oval, thus indicating that the Pharaoh's royal rights were also held by, and therefore derived from, God Himself. There was thus, as Christ later taught His disciples to believe, a kingdom of heaven over which God presided ; and although impersonal, intangible, and incomprehensible, the Aton was the very " Kings of kings, the only ruler of princes." Amon-Ra and other of the old deities had been called at various times " King of the gods." Akhnaton, however, applied to Aton the words " King and God."

Akhnaton is spoken of as " the unique one of Ra, whose beauties Aton created," and as " the

beloved son of Aton," whom "Aton bare."
Addressing the Aton, his courtiers were wont to
say, "Thy rays are on Thy bright image, the
Ruler of Truth (*i.e.*, the King), who proceeded
from eternity. Thou givest to him Thy duration
and Thy years; Thou hearkenest to all that is
in his heart, because Thou lovest him. Thou
makest him like the Aton, him Thy child, the
King." " Thou lookest on him, for he proceeded[1]
from Thee." "Thou hast placed him beside
Thee for ever and ever, for he loves to gaze upon
Thee. . . . Thou hast set him there till the
swan shall turn black and the crow turn white,
till the hills rise up to travel and the deeps rush
into the rivers." "While heaven is, he shall
be." Some of the Pharaohs had called themselves "the beautiful child of Amon"; and
Akhnaton, borrowing this phrase, was sometimes
spoken of as "the beautiful child of the Aton."[2]

In his capacity as Pharaoh and "son of God,"
Akhnaton demanded and received a very considerable amount of ceremonial homage; but
he never blinded himself to the fact that he was
primarily but a simple man. He most sincerely
wished that his private life should be a worthy
example to his subjects, and he earnestly desired

---

[1] Probably by royal descent is meant.

[2] In the tomb of a certain Amenhotep, at El Assasîf, temp. Amenophis III., the deceased Amenophis I. is called "The beautiful child
of Amon."

that it should be observed in all its naturalness
and simplicity. He did his utmost to elevate
the position of women and the sancity of the
family by displaying to the world the ideal conditions of his own married life. He made a point
of caressing his wife in public, putting his arm
around her neck in the sight of all men ; and in
a little ornament now in the possession of Colonel
Anderson, he is shown kissing his queen, their
lips being pressed together. As we have seen,
one of his forms of oath was, " As my heart is
happy in the Queen and her children. . . ."
He spoke of his wife always as " Mistress of his
happiness, . . . at hearing whose voice the
King rejoices."   " Lady of grace " was she,
" great of love " and " fair of face."   Every wish
that she expressed, declared Akhnaton, was
executed by him. Even on the most ceremonious
occasions the queen sat beside her husband and
held his hand, while their children frolicked
around them ; for such things pleased that
gentle Father more than the savour of burnt-
offerings. It is seldom that the Pharaoh is
represented in the reliefs without his family ;
and, in opposition to all tradition, the queen
is shown upon the same scale of size and importance as that of her husband. Akhnaton's
devotion to his children is very marked, and he
taught his disciples to believe that God was the

father, the mother, the nurse, and the friend of
the young. Thus, though " son of God," Akhnaton preached the beauty of the human family,
and laid stress on the sanctity of marriage and
parenthood.

6. THE CONNECTIONS OF THE ATON WORSHIP WITH OLDER RELIGIONS

In developing his religion Akhnaton must have
come into almost daily conflict with the priesthoods of the old gods of Egypt ; and even the
Heliopolitan Ra-Horakhti, from which his own
faith had been evolved, now fell far short of
his ideals. He does not seem, however, to have
yet imposed the worship of the Aton upon the
provinces, nor to have persecuted the various
priesthoods. He hoped, no doubt, that he would
be able to persuade the whole country to his
views as soon as those views were thoroughly
matured ; and, secure in his new city, he was
free to purge his religion of its faults before
declaring all other creeds illegal.

It is probable that the sacred bull, Mnevis,
was banished from his ceremonies at an early
date, for no tombs seem to have been made for
these holy creatures, and they are not referred
to after the sixth year of the king's reign. The
priests of Heliopolis would now have hardly
recognised their doctrines in the exalted faith

of the Aton, though here and there some point
of close contact might have been observed.   One
may also detect slight resemblances to the Adonis
religions of Syria, from whence the Aton had
originally come.   Mention has already been made
of the worship of Adonis.   So widespread was
that deity's power that it very naturally affected
many other religions.   In the Biblical Psalms
one finds several echoes of this old pagan worship,
as for example in the lines from Psalm xix, which
read :—

> The heavens declare the glory of God. . . .
> In them hath he set a tabernacle for the sun,
> Which is a bridegroom coming out of his chamber,
> And he rejoiceth as a strong man to run a race.
> There is nothing hid from the heat thereof.

Here one surely must recognise the youthful
Adonis, the bridegroom of Venus.   And similarly
in the Heliopolitan worship, at the commencement of Akhnaton's reign, the sun, Ra, is referred
to in the following terms : " Thou art beautiful
and youthful as Aton before thy mother Hathor
[Venus]."

In Akhnaton's religion one may still catch
a fleeting glimpse of Adonis.   One of the king's
courtiers, named May, held the office of " Overseer of the House for sending Aton to rest."[1]
Akhnaton's queen is mentioned in the tomb of

---

[1] So Prof. Breasted translates the Egyptian *sehetep*, though it
would be possible to give it other interpretations.

Ay under the peculiar title of " She who sends
the Aton to rest with a sweet voice, and with
her two beautiful hands bearing two systrums."
This " house " was, no doubt, the temple at
which the vesper prayers to the Aton were said
at sunset, and from the above title of the queen
it would seem that she had particular charge of
these evening ceremonies. One cannot contem-
plate the fact that it was a woman who officiated
at a ceremony which consisted of a lament[1] for
the departure of the sun without seeing in it
some connection, however faint, with the story
of Venus and Adonis. The lament of Venus for
the death of Adonis—*i.e.*, the setting of the sun
—was one of the fundamental ceremonies of the
Mediterranean religions. Here again was a connection with an older religion for Akhnaton to
consider and perhaps to purge away ; and one
may suppose that all such derivatives from
earlier faiths were gradually eliminated as the
young king developed his creed. Soon not a
scrap of superstition remained in the religion ;
and one may credit this Pharaoh of three thousand
years ago with as great a freedom from the
trammels of traditional superstition as that of
the advanced thinker of to-day.

[1] Cf. such expressions as " when thou settest they die," and
others used in Akhnaton's hymns.

7. THE SPIRITUAL NEEDS OF THE SOUL
AFTER DEATH

" Truly the light is sweet, and a pleasant thing
it is for the eyes to behold the sun," says Holy
Writ in words which might have fallen from
the lips of Akhnaton ; " but though a man live
many years and rejoice in them all, yet let him
remember the days of darkness, for they shall
be many." As Akhnaton had completely revolu-
tionised the beliefs of the Egyptians as to the
nature of God, so he altered and purged their
theories regarding the existence of the soul after
death. According to the old beliefs, as we have
seen, the soul of a man had to pass through
awful places up to the judgment throne of Osiris,
where he was weighed in the balances. If he
was found wanting he was devoured by a ferocious
monster, but if the scales turned in his favour
he was accepted into the Elysian fields. So
many were the spirits, bogies, and demigods
which he was likely to meet before the goal was
reached that he had to know by heart a tedious
string of formulæ, the correct repetition of which,
and the correct making of the related magic,
alone ensured his safe passage.

Akhnaton flung all these formulæ into the fire.
Djins, bogies, spirits, monsters, demigods, demons, and Osiris himself with all his court, were

swept into the blaze and reduced to ashes.
Akhnaton believed that when a man died his
soul continued to exist as a kind of astral, im-
material ghost, sometimes resting in the dreamy
halls of heaven, and sometimes visiting, in
shadowy form, the haunts of the earthly life.
By some of the inscriptions one is led to suppose
that, as in the fourth article of the Christian
faith, so in the teachings of Akhnaton, the body
was thought to take again after death its " flesh,
bones, and all things appertaining to the perfection of man's nature." But just as there is
some doubt and some vagueness in the mind of
Christian thinkers as to the meaning of this
article, so in Akhnaton's doctrine there was
some uncertainty as to whether the body was
entirely spiritual or in a manner material in its
hazy existence in the Hills of the West. The
disembodied soul still craved the pleasures of
earthly life and shunned its sorrows ; still felt
hunger and thirst and enjoyed a draught of water
or a meal of solid food ; still warmed itself in
the sunshine or sought coolness in the shadows.

We hear nothing of hell ; for Akhnaton, in
the tenderness of his heart, could not bring
himself to believe that God would allow suffering
in any of His creatures, however sinful. The
inscriptions seem rather to indicate that there
was no future life for the wicked—that they

were annihilated; though in almost every man
one may suppose that there was enough good
to recommend him to the mercy of a God so
loving as the Aton.

The first great wish of the deceased was that
he might each day leave the dim underworld in
order to see the light of the sun upon earth.
This had been the prayer of the Egyptians from
time immemorial, and to suit the religion of
the Aton its wording alone was changed. The
disciple of Akhnaton asked to be allowed "to
go out from the underworld in the morning to
see Aton as he rises." He prayed insistently,
passionately, in varied language, that his spirit
might "go forth to see the sun's rays," that his
"two eyes might be opened to see the sun,"
that there might be "no failure to see it," that
the "vision of the sun's fair face might never be
lost to him," that he "might obtain a sight of
the beauty of each recurring sunrise," and that
"the sun's rays might spread over his body."
Sometimes it is the Aton whom the soul thus
craves to see; sometimes it is Ra, the sun; but
always it seems to be the actual light and
warmth of the sunshine which is so passionately
desired. The abstract conditions of the future
life could but be interpreted in terms of human
experience; and in contemplating that cold,
desolate mystery of death, Akhnaton could find

no better means of banishing the gloom than by praying for a continuance of the blessed light of the day. And the man who prayed that his soul might see the sunshine but asked that he might still know the joy of the presence of God, for God was the light of the world.

His second wish was that he might retain the favour of the king and queen after death, and that his soul might serve their souls in the palaces of the dead. He asks for " readiness in the presence of the King " to do his bidding; he prays that he may be admitted into the palace, " entering it in favour and leaving it in love "; that he may " attend the King every day "; and that he may " receive honour in the presence of the King."

For his mental contentment in the underworld he earnestly desired that " his name might be remembered and established on earth," that there might be " a happy memory of him in the King's palace," and " a continuance of his name in the mouths of the courtiers," where he hoped that it " might be welcome." " May my name thrive in the tomb-chapel," he says. " May my name not be to seek in my mansion. May it be celebrated for ever." So, too, at the present day the words *In Memoriam* are goodly words; and that a man's memory may be kept green is a thing very generally desired.

8. THE MATERIAL NEEDS OF THE SOUL

In order that the soul might have its link with earth, the worshipper of the Aton prayed that his mummy might remain " firm " and uncorrupted, that the " flesh might live upon the bones," and that his limbs might remain " knit together." The Egyptians of other days believed that the body itself would live again at the resurrection, this being the reason why they attempted so carefully to preserve it ; and Akhnaton does not appear to have altered this conception of the nature of the material body. So, too, in the Christian faith it is thought that at the last day the graves will give up their dead.

The spiritual body retained the form and the individuality of the material body, and therefore, in a somewhat vague manner, it was thought that the needs of the soul would not be very dissimilar from those of the body upon earth. Christ, after His resurrection, asked for food ; and the feasts of Paradise are more than allegory to many a Christian. Likewise the follower of Akhnaton believed that material food, or its spiritual equivalent, would be necessary to the soul's welfare in the next world. " May I be called by my name," says he, " and come at the summons, in order to feed upon the good things provided upon the temple altar." It would seem

that through fidelity to the Aton creed he might
have the privilege of partaking of the offerings
made at the great ceremonies in the temple;
for, after these sacrifices had been offered, the
food, probably, was distributed to the priests
and to those attached to the tombs, who represented the interests of the dead. Thus the
deceased prays that he may enjoy " a reception
of that which has been offered in the temple";
" a reception of offerings of the King's giving in
every shrine"; " a drink-offering in the temple
of Aton"; " food deposited on the altar every
day"; and " everything that is offered in the
sanctuary of Aton in the City of the Horizon of
Aton." He further asks that " wine may be
poured out" for him, and that " the children of
his house may spill a libation for him at the
entrance of his tomb."

While life lasted God was very apparent to
those who sought Him. Wherever the sun shone,
wherever the great pulse of the earth beat
beneath one, wherever the river flowed or the
garden bloomed, there was God to be found;
for God was happiness, was beauty, was love.
But when the cold mists of death had enveloped
a man, when there was no longer any spring-
time nor any opening of the blossoms, how should
there be contentment any more? From the
depths of his heart Akhnaton urged his followers

to pray God that He might provide this happiness, though it could only be voiced in very human words. It was not "sweet perfume" nor "the smell of incense" that the soul required; but how else could the pleasure of light-heartedness be worded? They prayed that their "limbs might be provided with pleasure every day." In the stagnant air of the tomb they craved for the touch of the "sweet breeze," for "the breath of the pleasant airs of the north wind." They hoped in shadowy form to be able to visit the beloved scenes of their lifetime. "May I raise myself up and forget languor," prays one. "May I leave and enter my mansion," says another. "May my soul not be shut off from that which it desires. May I walk as I will in the grove that I have made upon earth. May I drink the water at the edge of my lake every day without ceasing." "May water be poured out from my cistern," cries a third; "may I receive fruit from my trees." Incessantly each man implores God to grant that he may cool his parched lips with water. "A draught of water at the banks of the river," is his desire; "a draught of water at the swirl of the stream." While he smells "the scent of the wind" blowing amidst the petals of "a bouquet of Aton," and while there runs "a brook of water" by his side, he need not know the horror of death. And thus,

by receiving " everything good and sweet," he
may hope for " health and prosperity " in the
hills and the valleys of the West ; for a " happy
life, provided with pleasure and joy," for " amusement, merriment, and delight," and for a " daily
rejoicing " throughout eternity.

It may be argued that this material conception
of the life after death is not equal in purity of
tone to the faith of the Aton. But is it, then,
less lofty to believe in a heaven in which there
is joy and laughter, a scent of flowers, and a
breath of north wind, than in one where the
streets are paved with gold, and where there are
many mansions ? By no religion in the world
is Christianity so closely approached as by
the faith of Akhnaton ; and if the Pharaoh's
doctrines as to immortality are not altogether
convincing, neither are the Christian doctrines,
as they are now interpreted, altogether without
fault. In the above pages it has been necessary
always to compare Akhnaton's creed with
Christianity, since there is so much common to
the two religions ; but it should be remembered
that this comparison must of necessity be un-
favourable to the Pharaoh's doctrine, revealing
as it does its shortcomings. Let the reader
remember that Akhnaton lived some thirteen
hundred years before the birth of Christ, at an
age when the world was steeped in superstition

and sunk in the fogs of idolatry. Bearing this
in mind, he will not fail to see in that tenderly
loving Father whom the boy-Pharaoh worshipped
an early revelation of the God to whom we of
the present day bow down ; and once more he
will find how true are the words—

"God fulfils Himself in many ways."

V

THE TENTH TO THE TWELFTH YEARS
OF THE REIGN OF AKHNATON

"One must be moved with involuntary admiration for the young
king who in such an age found such thoughts in his heart."—BREASTED
"History of Egypt."

1. THE HYMNS OF THE ATON WORSHIPPERS

IN the tombs of rich persons who had lived and
died previous to the time of Akhnaton, a large
portion of the walls had been covered with
religious inscriptions; and when at first the
nobles of the City of the Horizon of Aton were
planning their sepulchres they must have been
at a loss to know what to substitute for these
forbidden formulæ. Soon, however, it became
the custom to write there short extracts from
the hymns which were sung in the temples of
the Aton. In a few cases these inscriptions
supply us with a definite psalm, which, although
short, seems to be complete. In one tomb—
that of Ay—however, there is a copy of a much
more elaborate hymn; and it would thus seem

L

that there were two main psalms in use in the temples, a longer and a shorter version of the same composition.

It was not unusual for the Egyptians to compose hymns in honour of their gods, and a few such have been preserved to us upon the walls of the old temples. Like the Hebrew psalms of later date, they were not always of a very high moral tone. They are often but chants of victory, dealing in battles, in thunders, and in tempests, and glorying in the wrath of heaven. he longer hymn to the Aton, which is here given in full,[1] is quite unlike any of these compositions, and both in purity of tone and in beauty of style it must rank high amongst the poems of antiquity.

" Thy dawning is beautiful in the horizon of heaven,
O living Aton, Beginning of life !
When Thou risest in the eastern horizon of heaven,
Thou fillest every land with Thy beauty ;
For Thou are beautiful, great, glittering, high over the earth ;
Thy rays, they encompass the lands, even all Thou hast made.
Thou art Ra, and Thou hast carried them all away captive ;
Thou bindest them by Thy love.
Though Thou art afar, Thy rays are on earth ;
Though Thou art on high, Thy footprints are the day.

When Thou settest in the western horizon of heaven,
The world is in darkness like the dead.
Men sleep in their chambers,

---

[1] Professor Breasted's translation.

Their heads are wrapped up,
Their nostrils stopped, and none seeth the other.
Stolen are all their things that are under their heads,
While they know it not.
Every lion cometh forth from his den,
All serpents, they sting.
Darkness reigns,
The world is in silence :
He that made them has gone to rest in His horizon.

Bright is the earth, when Thou risest in the horizon,
When Thou shinest as Aton by day.
The darkness is banished
When Thou sendest forth Thy rays ;
The two lands [of Egypt] are in daily festivity,
Awake and standing upon their feet,
For Thou hast raised them up.
Their limbs bathed, they take their clothing,
Their arms uplifted in adoration to Thy dawning.
Then in all the world they do their work.

All cattle rest upon the herbage,
All trees and plants flourish ;
The birds flutter in their marshes,
Their wings uplifted in adoration to Thee.
All the sheep dance upon their feet,
All winged things fly,
They live when Thou hast shone upon them.

The barques sail up-stream and down-stream alike.
Every highway is open because Thou hast dawned.
The fish in the river leap up before Thee,
And Thy rays are in the midst of the great sea.

Thou art He who createst the man-child in woman,
Who makest seed in man,
Who giveth life to the son in the body of his mother,

Who soothest him that he may not weep,
A nurse [even] in the womb.
Who giveth breath to animate every one that He maketh.
When he cometh forth from the body . . .
On the day of his birth,
Thou openest his mouth in speech,
Thou suppliest his necessities.

When the chicken crieth in the egg-shell,
Thou givest him breath therein, to preserve him alive ;
When Thou hast perfected him
That he may pierce the egg,
He cometh forth from the egg,
To chirp with all his might ;
He runneth about upon his two feet,
When he hath come forth therefrom.

How manifold are all Thy works !
They are hidden from before us,
O Thou sole God, whose powers no other possesseth.
Thou didst create the earth according to Thy desire,
While Thou wast alone :
Men, all cattle large and small,
All that are upon the earth,
That go about upon their feet ;
All that are on high,
That fly with their wings.
The countries of Syria and Nubia
The land of Egypt ;
Thou settest every man in his place
Thou suppliest their necessities.
Every one has his possessions,
And his days are reckoned.
Their tongues are divers in speech,
Their forms likewise and their skins,
For Thou, divider, hast divided the peoples.

Thou makest the Nile in the nether world,
Thou bringest it at Thy desire, to preserve the people alive.
O Lord of them all, when feebleness is in them,
O Lord of every house, who risest for them,
O sun of day, the fear of every distant land,
Thou makest [also] their life.
Thou hast set a Nile in heaven,
That it may fall for them,
Making floods upon the mountains, like the great sea,
And watering their fields among their towns.

How excellent are Thy designs, O Lord of eternity !
The Nile in heaven is for the strangers,
And for the cattle of every land that go upon their feet ;
But the Nile, it cometh from the nether world for Egypt.
Thus Thy rays nourish every garden ;
When Thou risest they live, and grow by Thee.

Thou makest the seasons, in order to create all Thy works ;
Winter bringeth them coolness,
And the heat [the summer bringeth].
Thou hast made the distant heaven in order to rise therein,
In order to behold all that Thou didst make,
While Thou wast alone,
Rising in Thy form as Living Aton,
Dawning, shining afar off, and returning.

Thou makest the beauty of form through Thyself alone,
Cities, towns, and settlements,
On highway or on river,
All eyes see Thee before them,
For Thou art Aton [or Lord] of the day over the earth.

Thou art in my heart ;
There is no other that knoweth Thee,
Save Thy son Akhnaton.
Thou hast made him wise in Thy designs

And in Thy might.
The world is in Thy hand,
Even as Thou hast made them.
When Thou hast risen they live ;
When Thou settest they die.
For Thou art duration, beyond mere limbs ;
By Thee man liveth,
And their eyes look upon Thy beauty
Until Thou settest.
All labour is laid aside
When Thou settest in the west.
When Thou risest they are made to grow. . . .
Since Thou didst establish the earth,
Thou hast raised them up for Thy son,
Who came forth from Thy limbs,
The King, living in truth, . . .
Akhnaton, whose life is long ;
[And for] the great royal wife, his beloved,
Mistress of the Two Lands, . . . Nefertiti,
Living and flourishing for ever and ever."

2. THE SIMILARITY OF AKHNATON'S HYMN TO PSALM CIV

In reading this truly beautiful hymn one cannot fail to be struck by its similarity to Psalm civ. A parallel will show this most clearly :—

AKHNATON'S HYMN.

The world is in darkness like the dead. Every lion cometh forth from his den ; all serpents sting. Darkness reigns.

PSALM CIV.

Thou makest the darkness and it is night, wherein all the beasts of the forest do creep forth. The young lions roar after their prey; they seek their meat from God.

When Thou risest in the horizon . . . the darkness is banished. . . . Then in all the world they do their work.

All trees and plants flourish, . . . the birds flutter in their marshes. . . . All sheep dance upon their feet.

The ships sail upstream and down-stream alike. . . . The fish in the river leap up before Thee ; and Thy rays are in the midst of the great sea.

How manifold are all Thy works !. . . Thou didst create the earth according to Thy desire,—men, all cattle, . . . all that are upon the earth. . . .

Thou hast set a Nile in heaven that it may fall for them, making floods upon the mountains . . . and watering their fields. The Nile in heaven is for the service of the strangers, and for the cattle of every land.

Thou makest the seasons. . . . Thou hast made the distant heaven in order to rise therein, . . . dawning, shining afar off, and returning.

The world is in Thy hand, even as Thou hast made them. When thou hast risen they

The sun riseth, they get them away, and lay them down in their dens. Man goeth forth unto his work, and to his labour until the evening.

The trees of the Lord are full of sap, . . . wherein the birds make their nests . . . The high hills are a refuge for the wild goats.

Yonder is the sea, great and wide, wherein are . . . both small and great beasts. There go the ships. . . .

O Lord, how manifold are Thy works ! In wisdom hast Thou made them all. The earth is full of Thy creatures.

He watereth the hills from above : the earth is filled with the fruit of Thy works. He bringeth forth grass for the cattle and green herb for the service of men.

He appointed the moon for certain seasons, and the sun knoweth his going down.

These wait all upon Thee... When Thou givest them[food] they gather it; and when Thou live ; when Thou settest they die. . . . By Thee man liveth.

openest Thy hand they are filled with good. When Thou hidest Thy face they are troubled : when Thou takest away their breath they die.

In face of this remarkable similarity one can hardly doubt that there is a direct connection between the two compositions ; and it becomes necessary to ask whether both Akhnaton's hymn and this Hebrew psalm were derived from a common Syrian source, or whether Psalm civ is derived from this Pharaoh's original poem. Both views are admissible ; but in consideration of Akhnaton's peculiar ability and originality there seems considerable likelihood that he is the author in the first instance of this gem of the Psalter.

When the young Pharaoh composed this hymn he was probably neither much more nor less than twenty-two or twenty-three years of age—a period of life at which many of the world's greatest poets have written some of their fairest poems. One sees that he believed himself to be the only man to whom God had revealed Himself and the fact that he never admits that he was in any way taught to regard God as he did, but always speaks of himself, and is spoken of, as the originator and teacher of the faith, indicates that the ideas expressed in the hymn were

Akhnaton
From a statuette in the Louvre

(*See page* 179)

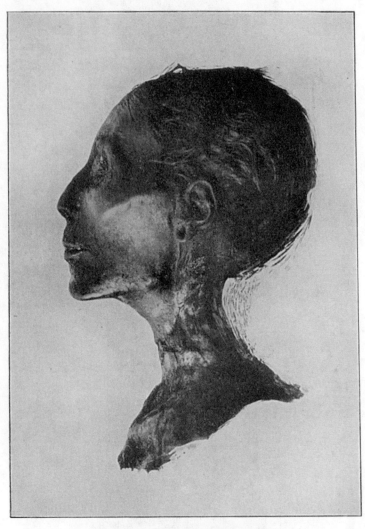

The Head of the Mummy of Thutmosis IV.,
the grandfather of Akhnaton

(*See page* 20)

The Mummy of Tuau, Grandmother of Akhnaton

(See page 20)

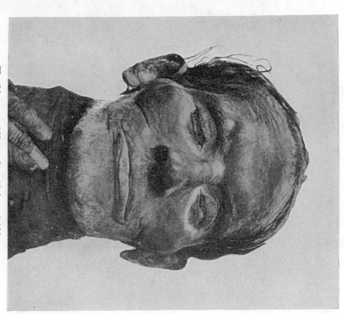

The Mummy of Yuaa, Grandfather of Akhnaton

(See page 28)

Site of the Palace of Akhnaton's Parents, at Thebes

(*See page* 31)

BORN - 1708
1698 - 10
88 - 20
78 - 30
68 - 40
58 - 50
7 - 51
6 - 52
1655 - 53

THUTMOSES IV

81 - BORN?
1680 - 1
79 - 2
78 - 3
77 - 4
76 - 5
75 - 6
65 - 16
1655 - 26
LIVED?
1681 — 1655
KING
1673 — 1655 (18)

Coffin of Yuaa
(*See page* 35)

Carved Wooden Chair, the designs partly covered with gold-leaf, found in the Tomb of Yuaa

(*See page* 35)

Chest belonging to Yuaa found in his Tomb

(*See page* 35)

Ceiling Decoration from the Palace of Akhnaton's parents, at Thebes

(*See page* 37)

Pavement Decoration from the Palace

(*See page* 37)

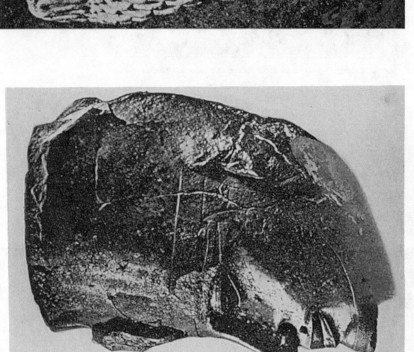

The Head of a Statuette of Akhnaton's Mother, Queen Tiy,
found by Professor Petrie in Sinai

(See page 43)

Amenophis III, the Father of Akhnaton
From the colossal statue in the British Museum

(See page 42)

The Head of Akhnaton from a Relief in the Temple of Luxor
(Colonnade of Horemheb)

(See page 58)

Alabaster Head of Akhnaton, from the lid of a
Canopic Jar found in his Tomb

(See page 232)

Akhnaton
From a Coloured Relief found at El Amarna

(*See page* 145)

Akhnaton
From his Statuette in the Louvre

(*See page* 179)

A Portrait Head of Akhnaton
found at El Amarna

(*See page* 180)

Fragment of a head of Akhnaton, now at Berlin
(From a drawing by the author)

(*See page* 180)

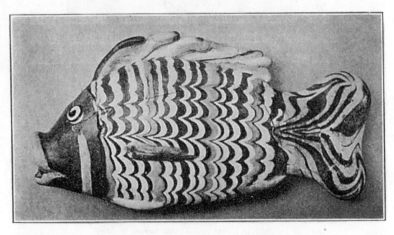

Vases of Varicoloured Glass found at El Amarna by
the Egypt Exploration Society

(*See page* 181)

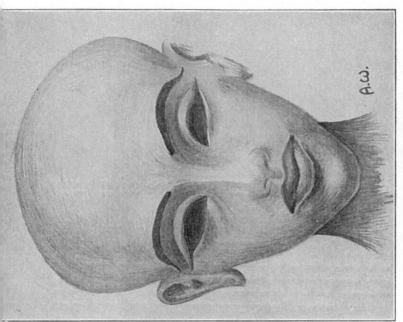

ANKHESENPAAMUN

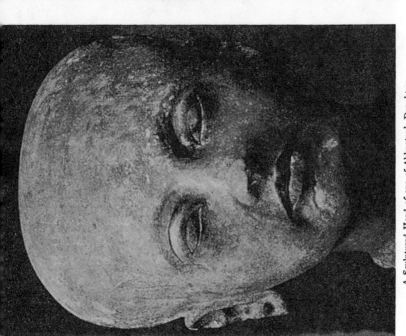

MERITATEN

A Sculptured Head of one of Akhnaton's Daughters,
found at El Amarna

(See page 185)

Head of one of Akhnaton's Daughters now in Berlin
(From a drawing by the author)

(See page 185)

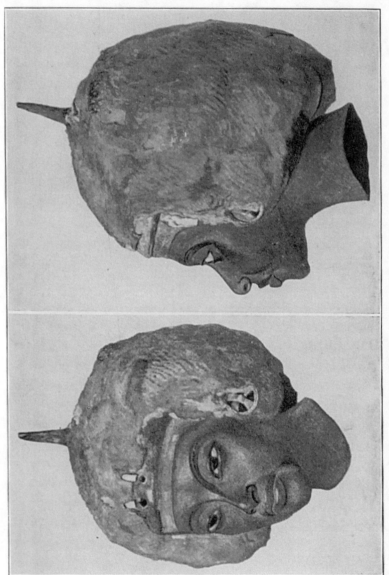

Head of a Statuette—perhaps of Queen Merytaton—now in Berlin

(See page 223)

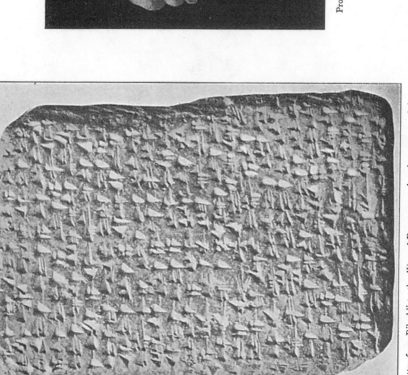

Probable Death Mask of Akhnaton, found by
Prof. Petrie at El Amarna.

(See page 229)

Letter from Ribaddi to the King of Egypt, reporting the progress of the
rebellion under Aziru. It is written in Cuneiform characters upon
a tablet of baked clay. (British Museum, No. 29,801.)

(See page 210)

Golden Vulture found upon Akhnaton's Mummy

(*See page* 229)

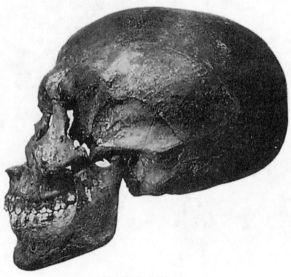

The Skull of Akhnaton

(*See page* 249)

entirely his own. The Aton religion was never
called by any other name than " The Teaching,"
a fact which suggests that the King himself was
the " teacher " of the new creed.

3. MERYRA IS MADE HIGH PRIEST OF ATON

The religion of the Aton had now assumed
shape and symmetry, and had been firmly established in the new capital as the creed of the court.
Akhnaton was thus able to intrust its administration and organisation there to one of his nobles
who had hearkened to his teaching, and to turn
his attention to other affairs, and more especially
to the conversion of the rest of Egypt. As head
of the state a thousand matters daily claimed
his consideration, and his high principles perhaps
led him to stray further along the by-paths of
administration than had been the wont of the
Pharaohs before him. His ill-health did not
permit him to tax his brain with impunity, and
yet there was never a king of Egypt before or
after him whose mind was so fruitful of thoughts
and of schemes. The young king himself ex-
pounded to his followers the doctrines which he
wished them to embrace, and one may suppose
that he sat for many an hour in the halls of
his palace, or under the trees in the gardens
beside the Nile, earnestly telling of the beauties
of the Aton to officials and nobles.

No one had accepted the king's teachings with greater readiness than a certain Meryra, who seems to have early associated himself with the movement; and it was to him that Akhnaton now handed over the office of " High Priest of the Aton in the City of the Horizon of Aton," in order to free himself for the great task of administering his kingdom and converting it to his way of thinking. Unfortunately we know very little of the career of Meryra, but on the walls of his tomb in the hills behind the capital there are a few reliefs which may here be described as illustrating events in his life and in the life of Akhnaton.

One of these scenes shows us the investiture of Meryra as High Priest. The king is seen with his wife and one of his daughters standing at a window of the gaily decorated *loggia* of the palace. The sill of the window is massed with bright-coloured cushions, and over these the royal personages lean forward to address Meryra and the company assembled in the pillared gallery outside. The outer surface of the *loggia* wall is brightly ornamented either with real or painted garlands of lotus-flowers, and with the many-coloured patterns usual upon such buildings in ancient Egypt. Ribbons, fluttering in the breeze, hang from the delicate lotus-pillars which support the roof, and vie in brilliancy with the red and blue ostrich-plume fans and standards carried by the officials.

Leaning from the window, with arm outstretched, Akhnaton bids Meryra rise from his knees, on to which he had cast himself on reaching the royal presence. Then solemnly the king addresses his favoured disciple in the following words :—" Behold, I make thee High Priest of the Aton for me in the Temple of the Aton in the City of the Horizon of Aton. I do this for love of thee, and I say unto thee : O my servant who hearkenest to the teaching, my heart is satisfied with everything which thou hast done. I give thee this office, and I say unto thee : thou shalt eat the food of Pharaoh, thy lord, in the Temple of Aton."

Immediately the asssembled company crowd round Meryra and lift him shoulder-high, while the new High Priest cries, " Abundant are the rewards which the Aton knows to give when his heart is pleased." The king then presents Meryra with the insignia of his office, and with various costly gifts, which are taken charge of by the servants and attendants who stand outside the gallery. Behind these attendants, at the outskirts of the scene, one observes the chariot which is to convey the High Priest back to his villa ; fan-bearers who shall run before and behind him ; women of the household who shall beat upon tambourines at the head of the procession, and who already dance with excitement as they see Meryra hoisted on to his friend's shoulder; and still other women who shall make the roadway rich with flowers.

This is no solemn and occult initiation of an ascetic into the mystery of the new religion, but rather the elevation of a good fellow to a popular post of honour. There was no mystery in the faith of the Aton. Frankness, openness, and sincerity were the dominant themes of Akhnaton's teaching—a worship of God in the blessed light of the day, the singing of merry psalms in the open courts of the temple; and the chosen High Priest was more likely to have been a deep-thinking, clean-lived, honest-hearted, God-fearing, family man, than an ascetic who had abandoned the pomps and the vanities of this world. The Pharaoh, while encouraging the Simple Life, did not preach the mortification of the flesh, but only the control of the body. The comforts of life, the brilliancy of decoration, the charms of music, the beauties of painting and sculpture, the pleasure of good company, the tonic of a bowl of wine, were all as acceptable to him, in moderation, as to the Preacher in Ecclesiastes.

4. THE ROYAL FAMILY VISIT THE TEMPLE

When Meryra had been installed, the king and royal family made a formal visit to the temple at the time of sunset, and this is likewise represented in the High Priest's tomb. For the first time in the history of Egypt one is permitted to see the Pharaoh as he drove through the streets of the capital in his chariot. No king before Akhnaton had allowed an artist to represent him in aught but celestial poses; but out of his love for truth and reality Akhnaton had dispensed with this convention, and encouraged the regarding of himself as a mortal man. On this occasion we see him standing in his gorgeously decorated chariot, reins and whip in hand, himself driving the two spirited horses, the coloured ostrich plumes on whose heads nod and toss as the superb animals prance along. The queen, also driving her own chariot, follows close behind; and after her again come the princesses, heading a noble group of chariots belonging to the court officials and ladies-in-waiting, these being driven by charioteers. The shining harness, the dancing red and blue plumes of the horses, the many-coloured robes, the feathered standards of the nobles, the fluttering ribbons, all go to make the cavalcade a sight to bring the townspeople running from their houses. A guard of soldiers, armed with spears, shields, battle-axes, bows, and clubs, races along on foot in front of the royal party to clear the road. Here, besides Egyptians, are bearded Asiatics from the king's Syrian dominions, befeathered negroes from the Mazoi tribes of Nubia, and Libyans from the west, wearing the plaited side-lock of hair hanging from their heads.

The party is seen to be nearing the temple, and Meryra stands before the gateway ready to greet his lord. Four men kneel near him holding aloft the coloured ostrich-plume fans, which will be wafted to and fro above the king's head when he has alighted from his chariot; and others kneel, lifting their hands in reverent salutation. Great bulls, fattened like the prize cattle of modern times, are led forth, garlands of flowers thrown around their huge necks, and bouquets of flowers fastened between their horns. These are attended by grooms, also bearing bunches of flowers. Two groups of female musicians, clad in flowing robes, wave their arms and beat upon tambourines.

The temple, which will be described later, is this day garlanded with flowers, and every altar is heaped high with offerings. Now the king has entered the building, and a further scene shows the royal family worshipping at the high altar, which is piled up with offerings of joints

of meat, geese, vegetables, fruit, and flowers,
surmounted by bronze bowls filled with burning
oil. Akhnaton and Nefertiti stand before the
altar, each with the right arm raised in the act
of sprinkling the fragrant gums of Araby upon
the flames. The upper part of the king's body
is bare, but from his waist depends a graceful
skirt of fine linen, ornamented with sash-like
ribbons of a red material, which flutter about
his bare legs. The queen's robe covers the whole
of her body, but is so transparent that one can
see her form with almost the distinctness of
nudity. A red sash is bound round her waist,
and the two ends fall almost to the ground.
Neither of the two wears any jewels ; and the
simplicity of the soft, flowing robes, with their
bright-red sashes, is extremely marked. Two
little princesses stand behind the king and queen,
each shaking from a systrum a note of praise
to God. Meryra, accompanied by an assistant,
stands bowing before the king, and near by
another priest burns some sweet-smelling incense.
Not far away there sits a group of eight blind
musicians—fat elderly men, who clap their
hands and sing to the accompaniment of a seven-
stringed harp, giving praise to the sunlight
which they cannot see, but yet can feel as " the
heat which is in Aton " penetrates into their
bones.

In still another series of reliefs we are shown a scene representing the reward of Meryra by Akhnaton on some occasion when he had been particularly successful in collecting the yearly dues of the temple from the estates on the opposite bank of the river. The ceremony took

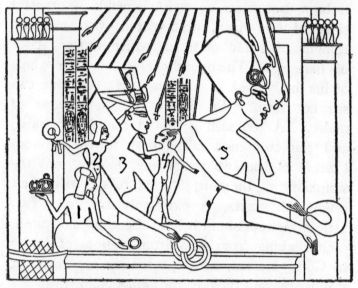

AKHNATON AND NEFERTITI WITH THEIR THREE DAUGHTERS,
throwing golden collars to a faithful noble of the court.

place in the granary buildings at the edge of the water. One sees a group of boats moored at the quay, and on the shore are several cattle-pens filled with lowing cattle. The granaries are stored with all manner of good things, and Meryra stands triumphant in front of them as the king addresses him.

① MERITATEN ② NEFRURE ④ ANKHSENE AHMUN ③ NEFERTITI ⑤ AKHENATEN

" Let the Superintendent of the Treasury of the Jewels take Meryra," says Akhnaton, " and hang gold on his neck at the front, and gold on his feet, because of his obedience to the teaching of Pharaoh " ; and immediately the attendants literally heap the gold collars and necklaces one above the other upon the High Priest's neck. Scribes write down a rapid summary of the events ; the attendants and fan-bearers bow low ; and Meryra is conducted back to his villa with music and with dancing, while Akhnaton returns to his palace, and, no doubt, sinks exhausted on to his cushions.

5. AKHNATON IN HIS PALACE

The reliefs and paintings upon the tombs often show the Pharaoh reclining thus, in a languid manner, as though the duties of his high calling had sapped all the strength from him. Never before had a Pharaoh been represented to his subjects in such human attitudes. The privacy of the palace is penetrated in these scenes, and we see the king, who loved to teach his followers the beauty of family life, in the midst of his own family. One or two of these representations must here be described. In one instance the royal family is shown inside a beautiful pavilion, the roof of which is supported by wooden pillars painted with many colours and having capitals

M

carved in high relief to represent wild geese
suspended by their legs, and above them bunches
of flowers. The pillars are hung with garlands
of flowers, and from the ceiling there droop
festoons of flowers and trailing branches of vines.
The roof of the pavilion on the outside is edged
by an endless line of gleaming cobras, probably
wrought in bronze.

Inside this fair arbor stand a group of naked
girls playing upon the harp, the lute, and the
lyre, and, no doubt, singing to that accompaniment the artless love-songs of the period.
Servants are shown attending to the jars of
wine which stand at the side of the enclosure.
The king is seen leaning back upon the cushions
of an arm-chair, as though tired out and sick
at heart. In the fingers of his left hand he
idly dandles a few flowers, while with his right
hand he languidly holds out a delicate bowl in
order that the wine in it may be replenished.
This is done by the queen, who is standing before
him, all solicitous for his comfort. She pours
the wine from a vessel, causing it to pass through
a strainer before flowing into the bowl. Three
little princesses stand near by : one¹ of them
laden with bouquets of flowers, another² holding
out some sweetmeat upon a dish, and a third³
talking to her father.

In another scene the king and queen are both

1 ANKHESENEAHMUN   2 NEFRURE   3 MERITATEN

shown seated upon comfortable chairs, while
a servant waits upon them.   The king is eating
a roasted pigeon, holding it in his fingers ; and
Nefertiti is represented drinking from a prettily
shaped cup.   The light, transparent robes which
they wear indicate that this is the midday meal ;
but unfortunately the painting is so much
damaged that nothing but the royal figures
remains.

6.   HISTORICAL EVENTS OF THIS PERIOD OF AKHNATON'S REIGN

There is very little historical information to
be procured for these years of the king's reign.
When he had been about ten or eleven years
upon the throne, and was some twenty-three
years of age, his fourth daughter, Neferneferuaton,
was born.   The queen had presented no son to
Akhnaton to succeed him, but he does not seem
in this emergency to have cared to turn to any
secondary wives ; and, as far as we can tell, he
remained all his life a monogamist, although
this was in direct opposition to all traditional
custom.   Steadily during these years the king's
health seems to have grown more precarious,
for almost daily he must have overtaxed his
strength.   His brain was so active that he could
not submit to be idle ; and even when he re-
clined amidst the flowers in his garden, his whole

soul was straining upwards in the attempt to pierce the barrier which lay between him and the God who had caused those flowers to bloom. The maturity of his creed at this period leads one to suppose that he had given to it his very life's force; and when it is remembered that at the same time his attention was occupied by the administration of a kingdom which he had twisted out of all semblance to its former shape, the wonder is that his brain was at all able to stand the incessant strain. Rare indeed must have been those idle moments which the artists of the City of the Horizon attempted to represent.

In the twelfth year of his reign, the tribute of the vassal kingdoms reached such a high value that a particular record was made of it, and scenes showing its reception were sculptured in the tombs of Huya and Meryra II.[1] An inscription beside the scene in the tomb of Huya reads thus :—

> Year twelve, the second month of winter, the eighth day. . . . The King . . . and the Queen . . . living for ever and ever, made a public

---

[1] In the tomb of Huya the scene is dated in the twelfth year, as here recorded, and there are four daughters shown, which is the number one is led by other evidence to suppose were then alive. The scene in the tomb of Meryra II has precisely the same date, but six daughters are shown, and there is evidence to show that that number is not to be looked for previous to the fifteenth year of the reign, the first daughter being born in about the fifth year, the second in the seventh, the third in the ninth, the fourth in the eleventh, the fifth in the thirteenth, and the sixth in the fifteenth

appearance on the great palanquin of gold, to receive the tribute of Syria and Ethiopia, and of the west and the east. All the countries were collected at one time, and also the islands in the midst of the sea ; bringing offerings to the King when he was on the great throne of the City of the Horizon of Aton, in order to receive the imposts of every land and granting them [in return] the breath of life.

The king and queen are shown seated in the state palanquin side by side ; and although Akhnaton holds the insignia of royalty, and is evidently very much upon his dignity, the queen's arm has found its way around his waist, and there lovingly rests for all the world to see. The palanquin, probably made of wood entirely covered with gold foil, is a very imposing structure : a large double throne, borne aloft by stout poles upon the shoulders of the court officials. The arm-rests are carved in the form of sphinxes, which rise above a glistening hedge of cobras, and the throne is flanked on either side by the figure of a lion carved in the round. A priest walks in front of the palanquin sending up a cloud of incense from a censer, and

year, in all probability. Thus the scene in Meryra II may perhaps represent no particular reception of the tribute of any one year, but the artist may have had in mind the great tribute of the twelfth year while representing the occurrence in the fifteenth or sixteenth year, at which date his work was taking place. Or again the date in this latter tomb may be a misreading or miswriting. The scene described above is that represented in the tomb of Meryra, as it is more elaborate than the other ; but the inscription is that found in the tomb of Huya.

professional mummers dance and skip in the roadway in advance of the procession. Behind the
royal couple walk the princesses, attended by
their nurses and ladies ; and on all sides are ar-
rayed courtiers, officers, soldiers, and servants.

Soon the ground marked out for the ceremony
is reached, and the king and queen betake them
selves to a gorgeous little pavilion which has been
erected for them, and here they sit together
upon a double throne, their feet supported upon
hassocks. The queen sits upon Akhnaton's left,
and in the picture her figure is hidden by that
of her husband ; but as her right arm is seen
to encircle his waist, and her left hand to hold
his left hand, one may suppose that she is reclining against him, with her royal head upon
his shoulder. Nefertiti was the mother of a
family of children, but was not more than about
twenty[1] years of age ; and one may presume that
this scene of conjugal affection was not without
its charm. The little princesses cluster round
the throne, one of them holding a young gazelle
in her arms, while another stroked its head.

In front of this pavilion the deputation from
the vassal kingdoms pass by ; and in order that
the king may not be wearied by their ceremonious homage, a group of professional wrestlers,

---

[1] Her first child, it will be remembered, was probably born when
she was about thirteen.

boxers, and fencers is provided for his diversion ;
while near them some buffoons and mummers
dance and tumble to the accompaniment of
castanets and hand-clapping. The tribute of
Syria is brought by long-robed Asiatics, who
cast themselves upon their knees before the
throne with hands uplifted in salutation. Splendid Syrian horses are led past, and behind
them chariots are wheeled or carried along.
Then come groups of slaves, handcuffed, but not
cruelly bound nor maltreated, as was the custom
under other Pharaohs. Bows, spears, shields,
daggers, elephant-tusks, and other objects, are
carried past and deposited upon the ground
near the pavilion ; while beautiful vases of
precious metal or costly stone are held aloft for
the king to admire. Wild animals are led across
the ground by their keepers, and amongst these
a tame mountain lion must have caused something of a sensation. Several nude girls, selected
probably for their beauty, walk past ; and one
may suppose that they will find subsequent
employment amongst the handmaidens in the
palace.

From the " islands in the midst of the sea "
come beautiful vases, some ornamented with
figures in the round. From Libya ostrich eggs
and ostrich feathers are brought. The tribute
of Nubia and the Sudan is carried past by

befeathered negroes, and consists mainly of bars and rings of gold and bags of gold-dust, procured from the mines in the Eastern Desert. Shields, weapons, tusks, and skins are also to be seen, and cattle and antelopes are led before the throne. As the Asiatics had startled the assembly by bringing with them a lion, so the negroes cause a stir by leading forward a panther of large size. Finally, male and female slaves, the latter carrying their babies in baskets upon their backs, are marched past the pavilion; but here again these slaves are not maltreated. It is particularly noticeable that the groups of miserable captives which one sees in all such scenes of other periods, with their arms bound in agonising positions and their knees giving way under them, are entirely absent from the representations of Akhnaton's ceremonies.[1] Human suffering was a thing hateful to the young Pharaoh who knew so well the meaning of physical distress; and the tortures of the prisoners, or the beheading of some rebel, such as would have been a feature of an occasion of this kind under Amenophis II, or even, perhaps, under Amenophis III, would have been as revolting to Akhnaton as it would be to us.

[1] The conventional design of captive figures of subject nations painted around the steps of the throne, is, however, to be seen in one of the El Amarna tombs, but this is not supposed to represent actuality.

7. QUEEN TIY VISITS THE CITY OF THE HORIZON

Akhnaton had left Thebes, as we have seen, in about the eighth year of his reign ; but his mother, Queen Tiy, seems to have been unwilling to accompany him, and to have decided to remain in her palace at the foot of the Theban hills. It is probable that she had not encouraged her son to create the new capital, and the removal of the court from Thebes must have been something of a grief to her, though no doubt she recognised the necessity of the step. In spite of advancing years she must have sorely missed. the pomp and circumstance of the splendid court over which she had once presided. Up to the fourth year of her son's reign, that is to say, until he had found his feet after coming of age at sixteen, she had been dominant, and the whole known world had bowed the knee to her. The luxuries of the many kingdoms over which she held sway had been hers to enjoy ; but now, with the king and the nobles gone to the City of the Horizon, and every penny which could be collected gone with them, the old queen must have been obliged to live a quiet, retired life in a palace which was probably falling into rapid ruin. Her little daughter, Baketaton, appears to have lived with her ; and it may be that some of her other daughters were still with her, though of them we hear nothing, and it is more probable that they had already died. It seems likely that she paid occasional state visits to her son, and permanent accommodation was provided for her in the City of the Horizon should she at any time desire to stay there. Her major-domo, an elderly man named Huya, appears to have lived for part of the year at the new capital, where a tomb was made for him ; and it is from the reliefs on the walls of this tomb that we obtain the knowledge of one of these state visits made by the old queen to Akhnaton. There is no evidence to show in what year the visit which forms the subject of the representations was made ; but as the twelfth year of Akhnaton's reign is mentioned in this tomb, it is probable that the visit took place somewhere about that time.

The queen must now have been between fifty and sixty years of age,[1] and her daughter Baketaton, born just before the death of her husband, was probably not much more than twelve years old. Akhnaton received his mother

[1] It is probable, as has been stated on p. 95, that she was married to Amenophis III in about her tenth year, and was thus about forty-six when he died. She could not have been much more, for her daughter Baketaton must have been born but a year or so before her husband's death, and it is improbable that she would bear children after forty-five, if as late as that.

and sister with apparent joy and festivity, and the major-domo, Huya, was called upon to organise many a *fête* in their honour. Some of them are shown in the reliefs, where even the conventionalities of the artist have not been able to hide from us the luxury of the scene. One sees Akhnaton, his wife Nefertiti, his mother Tiy, his sister Baketaton, and his two daughters Merytaton and Ankhsenpaaton, seated together on comfortable cushioned chairs, their feet resting on elaborate footstools. Akhnaton is clad in a skirt of clinging linen, but the upper part of his body seems to have been bare. On his forehead there gleams a small golden serpent, and on his feet there are elaborate sandals; but with customary simplicity he wears no jewellery. Queen Nefertiti wears a flowing robe of fine linen, and on her forehead also there is the royal serpent. Queen Tiy wears the elaborate wig which was in vogue during the days of the old *régime*, and upon it there rests an ornamental crown consisting of a disk, two horns, two tall plumes, and two small serpents, probably all wrought in gold. A graceful robe of some almost transparent material falls lightly over her figure. The little girls appear to be naked.

Around this happy family group there stand graceful tables upon which food of all kinds is heaped. Here are joints of meat, dishes of confectionery, vegetables, fruit,[1] bread, cakes of various kinds, and so on. The tables are massed with lotus-flowers, according to the charming custom of the ancient Egyptians of all periods. Beside the tables stand jars of wine and other drinkables, festooned with ribbons. At the moment selected by the artist for reproduction, Akhnaton is seen placing his teeth in the neatly trimmed meat adhering to a large bone which he holds in his hand. To this day it is the custom in Egypt thus to eat with the hands. Nefertiti has a small roast duck in her hands at which she daintily nibbles. Tiy's morsel cannot now be seen, but as she places it to her mouth with one hand she presents a portion to her daughter, Baketaton, with the other. The two little princesses feed by Nefertiti's side, and appear to be sharing the meal. Meanwhile Huya hurries to and fro superintending the banquet, carefully tasting each dish before it is presented to the royal party. Two string bands play alternately, the one Egyptian and the other apparently Syrian. The former consists of four female performers, the first playing on a harp, the second and third on lutes, and the fourth on a lyre. The main instrument in the foreign

[1] It is to be noticed that there are pomegranates amongst the fruit, which indicates that the visit was made during the summer. as do the light costumes also.

band is a large standing lyre, about six feet in height, having eight strings, and being played with both hands. Courtiers clad in elaborate dresses, and holding ostrich-plume standards, are grouped around the hall in which the banquet takes place.

Another set of reliefs in the tomb of Huya shows us an evening entertainment in honour of Queen Tiy. Again the same members of the royal family are represented, but against the cool night air more clothes are worn by each person, and the upper part of the king's body is now seen to be covered by a mantle of soft linen. The king, queen, and queen-dowager are all shown drinking from delicate bowls, probably made of gold. This being an evening festival, little solid food appears to have been eaten, but there are three flower-decked tables piled high with fruit. From these the little princesses, now wearing light garments, help themselves liberally ; and the small Ankhsenpaaton stands upon the footstool of her mother's chair, holding on to her skirts with one hand, while with the other she crams a plum or some similar fruit into her mouth. Two string bands make music as before, and again the groups of courtiers stand about the hall ; while Huya hastens to and fro directing the waiters, who, with napkins thrown over their arms, replenish the drinking-bowls from the wine-jars. The hall is lit by several flaming lamps set upon tall stands, near each of which these jars have been placed.

8. TIY VISITS HER TEMPLE

One more scene from this state visit is shown. Here we observe Akhnaton leading his mother affectionately by the hand to a temple which had been built in her honour, as her private place of worship, and which was called the "Shade of the Sun." This temple appears to have been a building of great beauty and considerable size. One passed through two great swinging doors fixed between the usual two pylons, and so entered the main court, which stood open to the sunlight. A pillared gallery passed along either side of this court, and between each of the columns there stood statues of Akhnaton, Amenophis III, and Queen Tiy. In the middle of the court rose the altar, to which one mounted by a flight of low steps. At the far end of the court another set of pylons and swinging doors led into the inner chambers. Passing through these doors one entered a small gallery, on either side of which there were again statues of the Pharaoh and his mother. Beyond stood the sanctuary, closed by swinging doors; and inside this was the second altar, flanked by statues of the king and queen-dowager. To

right and left of the sanctuary there were small
chapels; and a passage led round behind the
sanctuary to the usual shrines, where more royal
statues were to be seen.

The building seems to have been brilliant with
colours; and on this particular occasion the
altars were heaped up with offerings. Great jars
of wine, decked with garlands of flowers and
ribbons, stood in the shadow of the colonnades;
and meat, bread, fruit, and vegetables were piled
on delicate stands, ornamented with flowers.

Akhnaton and Tiy were accompanied by the
little Princess Baketaton, Akhnaton's sister, and
her two ladies-in-waiting. Before them walked
the queen's major-domo, Huya, accompanied by
a foreign official wearing what appears to be
Cretan costume.[1] Behind them walked a noble
group of courtiers bearing ostrich-plume fans
and standards; and outside the temple precincts
waited a crowd of policemen, servants, charioteers
and grooms in charge of the royal chariots, fan-
bearers, porters, and temple attendants. These
people shout and cheer loyally as the royal party
arrives. "The ruler of the Aton!" they cry.
"He shall exist for ever and ever!" "She who
rises in beauty!" "To him on whom the Aton
rises!" "She who is patron of this temple of
Aton!" The old queen must have felt as though

[1] Davies : Amarna, iii. 8, note 1.

she were back once more in the days of her
glory ; and yet how different the simplicity of
the religious ceremonies from those of the old
priests of Amon-Ra. There was now but a
prayer or two at the altar, a little burning of
incense, a little bowing of the head, and then
the procession back to the palace, and the silent
closing of the holy gates.

9. THE DEATH OF QUEEN TIY

It is possible that Queen Tiy took up her
residence at the City of the Horizon in recognition of the lavish arrangements which her son
had made for her. But whether this be so or
not, it does not seem that she lived very long
to enjoy such renewals of the pomps which she
had known in her younger days. Her death
appears to have taken place shortly after these
celebrations, and, probably by her express commands, she was embalmed at Thebes and carried
from her palace up the winding valley to the
royal burying-ground amongst the rugged Theban
hills. Akhnaton showed his affection for her by
presenting the furniture for the tomb, and in
the inscriptions on the outer coffin one reads
that " he made it for his mother." The queen-
dowager had evidently expressed a wish to be
buried near her father and mother, Yuaa and

Tuau ; for the tomb, which is situated on the east side of the valley, is within a stone's-throw of the sepulchre where they lay. It was entered by a steep flight of steps leading down to a sloping passage, at the end of which was the large burial chamber, the walls of which were carefully whitewashed. On passing into this chamber a great box-like shrine, or outer coffin, was to be found, occupying the greater part of the room. The door to the shrine was made of costly cedar of Lebanon covered with gold, and was fitted with an ornamental bolt. Many of the nails which held the woodwork together were made of pure gold—a fact which plainly shows us the wealth of the royal treasuries at this time. Scenes were embossed on the panels showing the queen standing under the rays of the Aton. The shrine itself was also made of cedar, covered with gold, and on all sides were scenes of the Aton worship. Here Akhnaton was shown with Tiy, and the life-giving rays of the sun streamed around their naturally drawn figures. Inside this outer box the coffin containing the great queen's mummy was laid. The usual funeral furniture was placed at the sides of the room : gaily coloured boxes, alabaster vases, faience toilet-pots, statuettes, &c. Some of the toilet utensils were made in the form of little figures of the grotesque god Bes, which

N

indicates that Akhnaton still tolerated the recognition by other persons of some of the old gods. In the inscriptions upon the outer coffin he had been careful to call his father, Amenophis III, by his second name, Nebmaara, as often as possible, in order to avoid the writing of the word Amon, his dislike of everything to do with that god being profound. He allowed it to be written, however, here and there, as it seemed right to him that it should appear. Akhnaton's prejudice against the old state god is also shown in another manner. Amon's consort was the goddess Mut " the Mother," whose name is written in hieroglyphs by a sign representing a vulture. Now when the inscription mentioned the king's *mother*, Tiy, the word *mut*, " mother," had to be written ; but in order to avoid a similarity—even in spelling—to the name of the goddess, Akhnaton had the word written out phonetically, letter by letter, and thus dispensed with the use of the vulture sign.[1] Again, in the name Nebmaara, the meaning of which is " Ra, Lord of Truth," the sign *maa*, " truth," represented the goddess of that name. Akhnaton's religion was much concerned with the quality of truth, which he regarded as one of the greatest necessities to happiness and well-

[1] This is to be observed also in some other inscriptions of the period.

being; and the fallacy of supposing that there was an actual deity of truth was particularly apparent to him. He was, therefore, careful to write the sign *maa* in letters instead of with the hieroglyph of the goddess.

When the funeral ceremonies came to an end, when the last prayer was said and the last cloud of incense had floated to the roof, the golden door of the shrine was shut and bolted, the outer doorways were walled up, and an avalanche of stones, let down from the chippings heaped near by, obliterated all traces of the entrance. Thus Akhnaton paid his last tribute to his mother and to the originator, it may be, of the schemes which he had carried into effect; and his last link with the past was severed. With the death of this good woman a restraining influence, as kindly as it was powerful, slipped from his arm, and a new and fiercer chapter of his short life began.

VI

THE THIRTEENTH TO THE FIFTEENTH YEARS OF THE REIGN OF AKHNATON

"The episode of the retirement of the king with his whole court to the new palace and city, . . . and the strange life of religious and artistic propaganda which he led there, . . . is one of the most curious and interesting in the history of the world."—BUDGE: "History of Egypt."

1. THE DEVELOPMENT OF THE RELIGION OF ATON

IN the Pharaoh's hymn to the Aton we read these words—

"Thou didst create the earth according to Thy desire, . .
The countries of Syria and Nubia,
The land of Egypt. . . ."

It is certainly worthy of note that Syria and Nubia are thus named before Egypt, and seem to take precedence in Akhnaton's mind. In the same hymn the following lines occur :—

"The Nile in heaven is for the strangers, . . .
But the Nile [itself], it cometh from the nether world for Egypt."

Here Akhnaton refers to the rain which falls in Syria to water the lands of the stranger, and compares it with the river which irrigates his own country. Thus again his thoughts are first for Syria and then for Egypt. This is the true imperial spirit : in the broadness of the Pharaoh's

AN EXAMPLE OF THE FRIENDLY RELATIONS BETWEEN SYRIA AND EGYPT.

A Syrian soldier named Terura, and his wife, attended by an Egyptian servant, who assists him to hold the tube through which he is drinking wine from a jar. From a tablet found at El Amarna. (Zeit. Aeg. Spr. xxxvi. 126.)

mind his foreign possessions claim as much attention as do his own dominions, and demand as much love. The sentiments are entirely opposed to those of the earlier kings of this dynasty, who ground down the land of the

" miserable " foreigner and extracted therefrom all its riches, without regard to aught else.

Akhnaton believed that his God was the Father of all mankind, and that the Syrian and the Nubian were as much under his protection as the Egyptian. The religion of the Aton was to be a world-religion. This is a greater advance in ethics than may be at once apparent; for the Aton thus becomes the first deity who was not tribal or not national ever conceived by mortal mind. This is the Christian's understanding of God, though not the Hebrew conception of Jehovah. This is the spirit which sends the missionary to the uttermost parts of the earth; and it was such an attitude of mind which now led Akhnaton to build a temple for the Aton in Palestine, possibly at Jerusalem itself, and another far up in the Sudan. The site of the Syrian temple is now lost, but the Nubian buildings were recently discovered and seem to have been of considerable extent.

At the same time temples were being erected in various parts of Egypt. At Hermonthis a temple named " Horizon of Aton in Hermonthis " was built; at Heliopolis there was a temple named " Exaltation of Ra in Heliopolis," and also a palace for the king; at Hermopolis and at Memphis temples were erected; and in the Fayoum and the Delta " Houses " of Aton sprang up. Few real converts, however, seem to have been made; for the religion was far above the understanding of the people. In deference to the king's wishes the Aton was accepted, but no love was shown for the new form of worship; and, indeed, not even in the City of the Horizon itself was it understood.

A certain change had been recently made by Akhnaton in the name of the Aton. The words " Heat which is in Aton " did not seem to him to be very happily chosen. They had been used in the earliest years of the movement, and perhaps had not been coined by Akhnaton himself. The word " heat " was in spelling very reminiscent of the name of one of the old gods, and, to the uninitiate, might suggest some connection. The name of the Aton was therefore changed to " Effulgence which comes from Aton," the new words introducing into the spelling the hieroglyph of Ra, the sun. The exact significance of the alteration is not known; but one may suppose that the new words better conveyed the meaning which Akhnaton wished to imply. Even now it is not easy to find a phrase to express that vital energy, that first cause of life, which the king so clearly understood.

The date of this change is somewhat uncertain, though it is definitely to be placed between the

ninth and twelfth year of the reign, the probability being that it took place in the ninth year,[1]
when Akhnaton was about twenty-five years
old. The inscriptions upon the outer coffin, or
shrine, of Queen Tiy show the new form of
wording, for the change had taken place when
her shrine was made.

2. AKHNATON OBLITERATES THE NAME OF AMON

Until this time it will have been observed
that Akhnaton had behaved with great leniency
towards the worshippers of the older gods, and
had not even persecuted the priesthood of Amon-
Ra. It now becomes apparent that this restraint
was due to his mother's influence, for shortly
after her death Akhnaton turned with the fierce-
ness of a fanatic upon the latter institution.
Possibly these Theban priests had attempted
a revolt, or had in some way caused the King to
take drastic steps. He issued an order that the
name of Amon was to be erased wherever it
occurred, and this order was carried out with such
amazing thoroughness that hardly a single occurrence of the name was overlooked. Although
thousands of inscriptions, accessible to Akhnaton's agents, are now known in which the
name of Amon occurs, there are but a few

[1] As Prof. Sethe has shown in an article published in 1921.

examples in which the god's name has not been
mutilated. His agents hammered the name out
on the walls of the temples throughout Egypt ;
they penetrated into the tombs of the dead to
erase it from the texts ; they searched through
the minute inscriptions upon small statuettes
and figures, obliterating the name therefrom ;
they made journeys into the distant deserts to
cut out the name from the rock-scribbles of
travellers ; they clambered over the cliffs beside
the Nile to erase it from the graffiti ; they entered
private houses to rub it from small utensils where
it chanced to be inscribed.

Akhnaton was always thorough in his under-
takings, and half-measures were unknown to
him. When it came to the question of his own
father's name, he seems not to have hesitated
to order the obliteration of the word Amon in
it, though one may suppose that in most cases
he painted over it the king's second name,
Nebmaara. His agents burst their way into
the tomb of Queen Tiy and removed the name
Amenophis from the inscriptions upon the shrine,
writing Nebmaara in red ink over each erasure.
Having scratched out the name even upon one
of the queen's toilet-pots of minute size they
retired from the tomb, building up the wall at
the entrance, and continued their labours elsewhere. The king was now asked whether his

own name, Amenophis—which had been used before he adopted the better known Akhnaton, —was to suffer the same fate, and the answer seems to have been in the affirmative. Upon the quarry tablet at Gebel Silsileh[1] the king's discarded name is thus erased, though it was not damaged in the tomb of Ramose. The names of the various nobles and officials, male and female, which were compounded with Amon— Amenhotep, Setamen, Amenemhet, Amenemapt, and so on—were ruthlessly destroyed; while living persons bearing such names were often obliged to change them.

In thus mutilating his father's name Akhnaton did not in any way intend to disparage his forbears. He was but desirous of utterly obliterating Amon from the memory of man, in order that the true God might the better receive acceptance. He was proud of his descent, and, unlike most of his ancestors, he showed a desire to honour the memory of his father. We have seen[2] how one of his artists, Bek, represented the figure of Amenophis III upon his monument at Aswan. Huya, Queen Tiy's steward, was authorised by Akhnaton to show that king upon the walls of his tomb;[3] and in the private temple of Queen Tiy, it will be remembered that there

[1] Page 54.
[2] Page 92.
[3] Davies : El Amarna, iii., Pl. xviii.

were statues of Amenophis III.[1] Likewise, the earlier kings of the dynasty received unusual recognition. An official named Any held the office of Steward of the House of Amenophis II.[2] and there is a representation of Akhnaton offering to Aton in " the House of Thutmosis IV in the City of the Horizon."[3] Upon his boundary tablet Akhnaton refers to Amenophis III and Thutmosis IV as being troubled by the priesthood of Amon.

It would seem from the above that there were shrines dedicated to Akhnaton's ancestors in the City of the Horizon, each of which had its steward and its officials ; and it is probable that Akhnaton arranged that a memorial shrine of the same kind should be erected ·for himself against his death, for we read of a personage who was " Second Priest " of the king,[4] and of another who was his " High Priest."[5] It was his desire in this manner to show the continuity of his descent from the Pharaohs of the elder days, and to demonstrate his real claim to that title " Son of the Sun " which had been held by the sovereigns of Egypt ever since the Fifth Dynasty, and which was of such vital importance in the

[1] Page 158.
[2] Davies : El Amarna.
[3] Wilkinson : Modern Egypt, ii. 69.
[4] Davies : El Amarna.
[5] Ashmolean Museum, Oxford.

new religion. It was in this manner that he
claimed descent from Ra, who was to him the
same with Aton ; and just as the great religious
teachers of the Hebrews made careful note of
their genealogies in order to prove themselves
descended from Adam, and hence in a manner
from God, so Akhnaton thus demonstrated the
continuity of his line in order to show his real
right to the titles " Child of Aton " and " Son
of the Sun."

3. THE GREAT TEMPLE OF ATON

The City of the Horizon of Aton must now
have been a very city of temples. There were
these shrines dedicated to the king's ancestors ;
there was the temple of Queen Tiy ; there was
a shrine for the use of Baketaton, the king's
sister ; there was the " House of putting the
Aton to Rest," where Queen Nefertiti officiated ;
and there was the great temple of Aton, in which
probably were included other of the buildings
named in the inscriptions. The great temple
may here be briefly described, as the reader has
so far made the acquaintance only of the building belonging to Queen Tiy.

The temple was entirely surrounded by a high
wall, and in this respect was not unlike the
existing temple of Edfu, which the visitor to
Egypt will assuredly have seen. Inside the

area thus enclosed there were two buildings, the one behind the other, standing clear of the walls, thus leaving a wide ambulatory around them. Upon passing through the gates of the enclosing wall there was seen before one the façade of the first of the two temples, while to right and left there stood a small lodge or vestry. The façade of the temple was most imposing. Two great pylons towered up before one, rising from behind a pillared portico, and between them stood the gateway with its swinging doors. Up the face of each pylon shot five tall masts, piercing the blue sky above, and from the heads of each there fluttered a crimson pennant. Passing through the gateway one entered an open court, in the midst of which stood the high altar, up to which a flight of steps ascended. On either side of this sun-bathed enclosure stood a series of small chapels or chambers; while in front of one, in the axial line, there was another gateway leading on into the second court, from which one passed again into a third court. Passing through yet another gateway, a fourth division of the temple was reached, this being a pillared gallery or colonnade where one might rest for a while in the cool shadow. Then onwards through another gateway into the fifth court, crossing which one entered the sixth court, where stood another altar in the full sunshine.

A series of some twenty little chambers were built around the sides of this court, and looking into the darkness beyond each of their doorways one might discern the simple tables and stands with which the rooms were furnished. A final gateway now led one into the seventh and last court, where again there was an altar, and again a series of chambers surrounded the open space.

Behind this main temple, and quite separate from it though standing within the one enclosure, stood the lesser temple, which was probably the more sacred of the two. It was fronted by a pillared portico, and before each column stood a statue of Akhnaton, beside which was a smaller figure of his wife or one of his daughters. Passing through the gateway, which was so designed that nothing beyond could be seen, one entered an open court in which stood the altar, and around the sides of which were small chambers. Here the temple ended, save for a few chambers of uncertain use, approached from the ambulatory.

Both buildings were gay with colours, and at festivals there were numerous stands heaped high with flowers and other offerings, while red ribbons added their notes of brilliant colour on all sides. There was nothing gloomy or sombre in this temple of Aton ; and it contrasts strikingly with the buildings in which Amon was worshipped. There vast halls were lit by minute windows, and a dim uncertainty hovered around the worshipper. Such temples lent themselves to mystery, and amidst their gloomy shadows many a supplicant's heart beat in terror. Dark stairways led to subterranean passages, and these passages to black chambers built in the thickness of the wall, from whence the hollow voice of the priest throbbed as from mid-air upon the ears of the crouching congregation. But in Akhnaton's temple each court was open to the full blaze of the sunlight.[1] There was, there could be, no mystery; nor could there be any terror of darkness to loosen the knees of the worshipper. Akhnaton had no interest in incantations and mysteries. Boldly he looked to God as a child to its father; and having solved what he deemed to be the riddle of life, there was no place in his mind for aught but an open, fearless adoration of the Creator of that vital energy which he saw in all things. Akhnaton was the sworn enemy of the tableturners of his day, and the tricks of priestcraft, the stage effects of religiosity, were anathema to his pure mind.

4. THE BEAUTY OF THE CITY

The City of the Horizon of Aton was now a place of surpassing beauty. Eight or nine years

[1] It is probable that there was some likeness between Akhnaton's temples and those dedicated to the sun in early days, as, for example, that at Abusèr.

of lavish expenditure in money and skill had transformed the fields and the wilderness into as fair a city as the world had ever seen. One of the nobles who lived there, by name May, describes it in these words : " The mighty City of the Horizon of Aton, great in loveliness, mistress of pleasant ceremonies, rich in possessions, the offering of the sun being in her midst. At the sight of her beauty there is rejoicing. She is lovely and beautiful : when one sees her it is like a glimpse of heaven."

Besides the temples and public buildings the city was adorned with numerous palaces, each standing in fair gardens. One of these mansions,[1] represented in the tomb of Meryra, seems to have constituted a happy combination of comfort and simplicity, as may be seen from its pictures. One entered a walled court, and so passed to the main entrance of the house. A portico, the roof of which was supported by four decorative columns festooned with ribbons, sheltered the elaborate doorway from the sunshine. Passing through this doorway, from the top of which a row of cobras gleamed down upon one, a pillared hall was reached ; and beyond this the visitor entered the great dining-hall. Twelve columns supported the ceiling, which was probably painted with flights of birds ;

---

[1] Perhaps this is a part of the royal palace.

and under a kind of kiosk in the middle of the hall stood the dining-table and several comfortable arm-chairs, cushioned in bright colours. Beyond this hall there was a court, at the back of which were several chambers, one being a bedroom, as a great cushioned bedstead clearly shows. The owner's womenfolk probably occupied another portion of the building not shown in the representations.

The palace of Ay, Akhnaton's father-in-law, was a more pretentious building. It was entered by a fine doorway which led into a court. A second door gave entrance to the large, pillared dining-hall, and through this one passed into a court from which bedrooms and boudoirs led off. In one of these rooms two women, clad in airy garments, are seen to be dancing with one another, while a man plays a harp. In another room a girl likewise dances to the strains of a harp, while a servant dresses the hair of one of the gentlemen of the household. Other rooms contain lutes, harps, and lyres, as well as objects of the toilet. A little court is now reached, where fragrant flowers grow, and tanks of water, sunk in the decorated pavement, give a sense of coolness to the air. Beyond this are more apartments, and finally the kitchens are reached. Throughout the house stand delicate tables upon which jars of wine or dishes of fruit are to be

o

seen ; and cushioned arm-chairs, with footstools before them, are ready for the weary. Servants are seen passing to and fro bearing refreshments, or stopping to dust the floor, or again idly talking in the passages.

Akhnaton's palace is not very clearly shown in the tomb reliefs or paintings, but portions of it were found in the modern excavations on the site. Like all the residential buildings of the period, it was an airy and light structure made of brick. The walls, ceilings, and floors were covered with the most beautiful paintings, and delicate pillars, inlaid with coloured glass and stone, or covered with realistically painted vines and creepers, supported the light ceilings of its halls. Portions of the pavement are still preserved, and the visitor to the site of the city may still see the paintings there depicted. A young calf, frisking in the sunlight, gallops through a field of red poppies ; wild geese rise from the marshes and beat their way through the reeds, disturbing the butterflies as they do so ; amidst the lotus-flowers resting upon the rippling water the sinuous fish are seen to wander. These are but fragments of the paintings which once delighted the eyes of the Pharaoh, or brought a sigh to the lips of his queen.

The art of the painter of this period excels in

the depiction of animal and plant life. The winding, tangled stems and leaves of vines were carefully studied ; the rapid motions of animals were correctly caught ; and it has been said that in these things the artists of Akhnaton were

THE ARTIST AUTA,
at work on a statuette of Baketaton.

greater than those in any other Oriental art.[1] Sculpture in the round, too, reached a pitch of excellence never before known. The statue of Akhnaton illustrated in the frontispiece is the work of one who may rank with Donatello; and

[1] Petrie : History of Egypt, ii. 219.

the bust of Nefertiti now in Berlin is perhaps the most lifelike portrait in all Egyptian art.

In the tomb of Huya there is a scene representing an artist named Auta, seated in his studio giving the final touches to a statue of Princess Baketaton. He sits upon a low stool, palette in hand, and, as was the custom, colours the surface of the statue. Unlike the stiff conventional poses of earlier work, the attitude of the young girl is easy and graceful. One hand hangs by her side : in the other she holds a pomegranate, which she is about to raise to her lips. Auta's assistant stands beside the figure, and near by two apprentices work upon objects of less importance, their chisels on a table by their side. The studio of another sculptor named Thutmose was found recently, and in it a number of beautiful busts came to light, some of which are here illustrated.

Works such as these which Thutmose, Auta, and their companions were turning out are permanent memorials of the reign of Akhnaton, which will carry his name through the years until, as he would say, " the swan turns black and the crow turns white." There must surely come a time, and soon, when the art of Egypt will receive more attention ; and one may then hear Akhnaton's name coupled with that of the Medici as the patron, if not the teacher, of great masters. It was he who released them from convention, and bade their hands repeat what their eyes saw ; and it was he who directed those eyes to the beauties of nature around them. He, and no other, taught them to look at the world in the spirit of life, to infuse into the cold stone something of the " effulgence which comes from Aton " ; and, if these few treasures which have survived the utter wreck of the City of the Horizon have put one's heart to a happy step, it was Akhnaton who first set the measure.

The excavations now (1922) being conducted by the Egypt Exploration Society on the site of the city have laid bare the remains of palaces and gardens which must have been of great beauty. There is, for instance, the " Precinct of Aton," a sort of sacred pleasure-garden, wherein the beauties of nature were gathered as though in living illustration of the oft-repeated words of the Aton hymns—" O Lord, how manifold are all Thy works; how excellent are Thy designs, O Lord!"

This " Precinct " consists of two large, walled enclosures, the first of which was entered through a hall of thirty-six columns, beyond which there was a small artificial lake set amidst trees and shrubs, the stumps and roots of which are still to be seen, planted in beds of earth which had been brought up into the sandy desert from the banks of the Nile. This lake seems to have been stocked with fish, and the roots and withered remains of the lotus-flowers and water-lilies which graced its surface have been found. At one side of this enclosure there are a series of buildings which appear to have been used as a sort of home-farm wherein were housed the cattle, sheep, ducks, and so forth, described in the Aton hymns as ever giving praise to God.

In the second enclosure, which leads from the first, there was a larger lake, again surrounded by gardens, and having a little quay built out into it, as though pleasure-boats had been used upon the water. There were beautiful summer-houses or kiosks in the garden, and along the north edge of the lake a fine colonnade was built, where one might sit in the shade to gaze upon the splendour of the sun reflected in the still water. Near by there were wine cellars, two of which were found still sealed up and containing wine-jars marked with the date of the vintage and its quality. " Very good wine " is written on certain of these jars.

In a corner of this enclosure there was a peculiarly beautiful little kiosk, the columns of which rose from out sunken tanks of water once filled with lotus-flowers. The walls and pillars were decorated with painted clusters of purple grapes and red pomegranates, blue lotus-flowers and green leaves ; and wild ducks were depicted flying upwards into the azure sky. A path, flanked by flower beds, led to another little lake wherein was an island approached by an ornamental bridge. On this island there was a summer-house decorated with faience tiles and charmingly painted designs.[1]

Several of the palaces and villas of the nobles have been laid bare in these amazing excavations, most of them being built along the two main avenues of the city, known as the Street of the High Priest and the King's Highway; and a brief description may here be given of one of these houses—that of Akhnaton's Vizier, Nakht. The building stands upon a raised platform, and the front door is approached by a flight of steps. A two-columned lobby and vestibule lead to the North Loggia, which is a sort of hall or verandah having large open casements overlooking the gardens. The ceiling, painted a brilliant blue, is supported by eight decorated wooden columns set on stone bases; the walls are vivid white with a frieze of blue lotus-flowers on a green ground; and the floor is of painted tiles. A doorway at each end of the Loggia leads into service rooms, and through another in the middle the Central Hall is approached. This

[1] The sand of the desert has blown over the ruins of the city to the depth of a few feet, and the excavators have but to remove this soft covering to reveal the well-preserved remains of all such gardens and the lower parts of walls and columns.

Hall, some thirty feet square, had four stone columns to support its elaborately decorated ceiling. Along one side a low divan was built, and upon this, no doubt, rugs and cushions were placed. In front of it there was a circular hearth set in a depression in the floor; and here a fire burned during the cold winter evenings, the smoke passing out through windows near the roof. In another part of the Hall there was an ablution platform of stone, where the Vizier or his guests stood while their hands and feet were washed by servants in the usual Oriental manner.

Four doors lead from this Hall to the inner rooms, including the Vizier's bedroom, wherein the bed stood upon a raised dais; to the West Loggia, which caught the afternoon sun, so pleasant in winter, and afforded cool morning shade in the hot weather; and to the stairs which ascended to the now destroyed upper floors and flat roof. Near the bedroom was the bathroom, where the bather stood upon a stone slab while water was poured over him by his servants, the waste draining away into a sunken basin. Next door to the bathroom was the chamber in which there was an earth-closet.

Houses such as these were each surrounded by gardens in which were charming little kiosks, and probably a small lotus-pond. Granaries and store chambers stood near the whitewashed enclosing-wall, and there was usually a well from which the household water-supply was drawn.

5. AKHNATON'S AFFECTION FOR HIS FAMILY

In about the thirteenth year of the reign a fifth daughter was born, who was named Nefer-neferura. It is significant that the name of Aton, of which all the previous daughters' names had been compounded, now gives place to Ra. A sixth daughter seems to have made her appearance somewhat over a year later, some time during the fourteenth year of the reign. Again Ra is used in the name instead of Aton, she being called Setepenra. It is impossible to say what was the meaning of this slight change in the theological aspect of the religion at this period, but it seems evident that certain developments in which Ra figured were now introduced.

No son was yet forthcoming, and both the king and the queen must now have suffered six successive disappointments. It may be mentioned here that the next child born to the unfortunate couple in the following year proved to be a seventh girl and a seventh disappointment; and in the remaining two years of the reign no other child was born, or at any rate was weaned, so that Akhnaton died sonless. It is strange to picture this lofty-minded preacher in his home, with his six little girls around him, as he is shown upon the monuments. No other Pharaoh thus portrayed himself surrounded by his family; but Akhnaton seems to have never been happy unless all his children were with him and his wife by his side. The charm of family life, and the sanctity of the relationship of husband and wife, parents and children, seems to have been an important point of doctrine to him. He urged his nobles, also, to give their

AKHNATON AND HIS WIFE AND CHILDREN.

attention to their families; and in the tomb of Panehesy, for example, one may see representations of that personage sitting with his wife and his three daughters around him. A little statuette, now in Berlin, shows the king seated upon his throne, and nursing one of his little daughters upon his knees. He is in the act of kissing her, and their lips are in contact—an intimate attitude which is all the more amazing when one remembers the usual severity and

restraint shown in Egyptian statuary of other
periods.

The King of Babylon, Burraburiash, wrote to
Akhnaton in about the fourteenth or fifteenth
year of the reign, asking for one of the Pharaoh's
daughters as a wife for his son. Wishing to be
on friendly terms with Babylonia, Akhnaton
consented to the union, and selected probably
his fourth daughter, Neferneferuaton, as the
future Queen of Babylon. His eldest daughter
subsequently married a noble named Smenkhkara,
who succeeded to the throne after the death of
Akhnaton ; and his third daughter was later
married to another noble named Tutankhaton,
who usurped the throne, as we shall see in the
sequel. The fact that neither of these daughters
was now chosen to marry the Babylonian prince
indicates that they were already betrothed to
their future husbands, and hence this event could
not have taken place much earlier than the
date mentioned above. The second daughter,
Meketaton, was not selected for the reason that
she seems to have been in a precarious state of
health. The little princess who was chosen was
born in the tenth year of the reign, and was now
not more than five years of age. Akhnaton did
not at once send the child to her future home,
but arranged the marriage by proxy, and thus
kept his daughter with him for yet a few years.

This is made evident from the fact that in a letter from Burraburiash to Akhnaton, the Babylonian king states that he is sending a necklace of over a thousand stones to the " Pharaoh's daughter, the wife of his son," who is thus evidently still resident in Egypt.

Besides Akhnaton's six, and presently seven, daughters there were two other princesses probably in residence at the palace. One of these, his young sister Baketaton, whom we have seen visiting the City of the Horizon with her mother, is not again heard of, and perhaps did not long survive the dowager-queen's death. The other was Nezemmut, the sister of Queen Nefertiti, who had probably married some Egyptian noble. Her portraits are shown in the tombs of May, Panehesy, and Ay ; and she is generally seen to be accompanied by two female dwarfs, named Para and Reneheh, who appear to have waddled after her wherever she went. She was still, no doubt, very young, and these two grotesque attendants were entrusted with her safety as well as her amusement.

6. AKHNATON'S FRIENDS

The simple and homely manner in which Akhnaton is represented by his artists, surrounded by his children, is an indication that although he demanded much homage from his

NEZEMMUT (OR MUTNOME) WIFE of HOREMHEB! DAU. of AYE!

subjects in his capacity as their Pharaoh, he but asked for their sympathy and affection in all other connections. As Pharaoh his person was inapproachable and his attitude aloof, but as a man he never failed to set an example of what he considered a man should do ; and even upon his throne, to which one might but advance with bowed head and bended knee, he displayed his mortal nature to all beholders by joking with his children or paying fond attention to his wife. So, also, many of his disciples and courtiers, who so ceremoniously approached the steps of his throne, were in reality his good friends and intimates. Akhnaton did not care very much for aristocratic traditions, and although he demanded the conventional respect of his subjects, and upheld the less tiresome rules of court etiquette, many of his closest friends were of peasant origin, and the hands which now held the jewelled ostrich-plume standards could as easily grasp the pick or the plough.

May, a high official of the city, speaks of himself in the following words : " I was a man of low origin both on my father's and on my mother's side, but the King established me. . . . He caused me to grow . . . by his bounty when I was a man of no property ; . . . he gave me food and provisions every day, I who had been one that begged bread." Huya, Queen Tiy's

steward, speaks of the king as selecting his officials
from the ranks of the yeomen. Panehesy tells
us that Akhnaton is one " who maketh princes
and formeth the humble," and he adds : " When
I knew not the companionship of princes I was
made an intimate of the King." But if the
Pharaoh raised men from the ranks, he was also
capable of degrading those who offended against
the standards which he had set up. Thus May
seems to have been disgraced and turned out of
the city.

The tomb of the police official, Mahu, who
was a favourite of the king, though probably
not of exalted origin, has provided us with some
scenes relating to his official work which are of
considerable interest. In one series of these we
are shown the capture of some foreigners, or
perhaps Beduin, who may have belonged to some
gang of thieves or rebels. Mahu has been
awakened in the early hours of a winter morning
by the news of the disturbance, and as he listens
to the report a servant blows a small fire into
flame, since the morning air is chilly. He then
sends for his chariot and drives to the scene of
the crime, whatever it may be ; and soon he has
effected the arrest of some of the culprits.
These men are then conveyed to the Vizir, who,
with his staff, receives Mahu with exclamations
of approval. " Examine these men, O Princes,"

says the police officer, "whom the foreigners have instigated." From these words it might seem that the prisoners were foreign spies, or even assassins plotting against the life of the Pharaoh.

Whether from fear of a revolt in Egypt or from mere custom, the City of the Horizon was closely defended at this time, and there is a scene in this same tomb in which Akhnaton is shown inspecting the fortifications. He drives in his chariot with his wife and his eldest daughter Merytaton; and although the spirited horses would appear to be difficult to manage, the more so because the mischievous Merytaton is poking them with a stick, Akhnaton is a sufficiently good driver to be able to carry on a conversation with the queen, and to address a few words to Mahu, who runs by the side of the chariot. In striking contrast to the custom of other Pharaohs, Akhnaton is accompanied by an unarmed bodyguard of police as he drives round the defences; and in this we may perhaps see an indication of his popularity. The fortifications, it may be noted, consist of blockhouses built at regular intervals, and defended by rope entanglements.

In several of the tombs there are representations of their owners receiving rewards from the king for their diligence in their official works,

or for their intelligent acceptance of his teaching.
A high official named Pentu has left us a scene
in which Akhnaton is shown seated in the hall
of his palace, while Pentu stands before him to
receive numerous golden collars at the royal
hands in recognition of his services. A part of
the palace is shown, but the scene is much
damaged : a small pond or tank surrounded by
flowers is shown in one corner of the enclosure,
but the plan of the various rooms is confused,
and is quite subsidiary to the representation of
the hall where the Pharaoh receives the happy
Pentu. Akhnaton seems to have been a good
friend, as he was a stern enemy ; and those who
assisted him in the difficult tasks which he had
set himself were lavishly rewarded for their
pains.

7. AKHNATON'S TROUBLES

Akhnaton's health was so very uncertain that
he hastened to construct for himself a tomb
in the cliffs behind the City of the Horizon.
He selected as the site of his last resting-place
a gaunt and rugged valley which here cuts into
the hills, leading back, around tumbled rocks
and up dry watercourses, to the Arabian desert
beyond. It is

"A savage place !— as holy and enchanted
As e'er beneath a waning moon was haunted
By woman wailing for her demon-lover."

Here Akhnaton elected to be buried, where
hyænas prowled and jackals wandered, and where
the desolate cry of the night-owls echoed over
the rocks. In winter the cold wind sweeps
up this valley and howls around the rocks; in
summer the sun makes of it a veritable furnace
unendurable to men. There is nothing here
to remind one of the God who watches over
him, and the tender Aton of the Pharaoh's conception would seem to have abandoned this place
to the spirits of evil. There are no flowers where
Akhnaton cut his sepulchre, and no birds sing;
for the king believed that his soul, caught up
into the noon of Paradise, would be freed from
the tomb.

The sepulchre consisted of a passage descending
into the hill, and leading to a rock-cut hall, the
roof of which was supported by four columns.
Here stood the sarcophagus of pink granite in
which the Pharaoh's mummy would lie. The
walls of this hall were covered with scenes carved
in plaster, [1] representing various phases of the
Aton worship. From the passage there led
another small chamber beyond which a further
passage was cut, perhaps to lead to a second
hall in which the queen should be buried; but
the work was never finished.

[1] The plaster has now fallen off, and little of the original decoration
remains. The tomb is seldom visited by tourists, being seven miles
back from the river; but it is in charge of the Government custodian.

P

The construction of the tomb was interrupted by the death of Akhnaton's second daughter, Meketaton, who had barely lived to see her ninth birthday. It has already been seen that she seems to have been ailing for some time, and her death was perhaps no surprise to her parents. Their grief, however, was none the less acute for this; and when the body of the little girl had been laid to rest in one of the chambers of her father's tomb, the walls were covered at Akhnaton's order with scenes representing the grief of the bereaved family. Here Queen Nefertiti is seen holding in her arms her lately born seventh daughter, whose name, ending in . . . t, is now lost; while the five other little girls weep with their parents beside the bier of their dead sister. It is a pathetic picture and one which stirs our sympathy for a Pharaoh who, unlike other kings of Egypt, could weep for the loss of a daughter. ⅄

This was not Akhnaton's only grief. His doctrines were not being accepted in Egypt as readily as he had hoped, and he was probably able to detect a considerable amount of insincerity in the attitude of those around him. There was hardly a man whom he could trust to continue in the faith should he himself die; and even as he put the last touches to his temples and his palaces he was aware that he

✗ SEE PAGE 256 !

had built his house upon the sand. The empire which he had dreamed of, bound together by the ties of a common worship of Aton, was fast fading out of sight, and the news which reached him from Syria was disquieting in the extreme.

At this time the King of Babylon, whose son had married Akhnaton's daughter, seems to have been on bad terms with his neighbour, the King of Mitanni, and Akhnaton came nigh to being drawn into the quarrel. The Babylonian king had been ill for some time, and in the course of the international correspondence Nefertiti had never sent her condolences to him. This was much resented, and the King of Babylon at last sent an insulting letter to Akhnaton, in which he states that he is sending him the usual present of decorative objects which etiquette required of him, but that he wishes it to be understood that only a fraction of the gift is intended for the " mistress of his house," *i.e.*, Nefertiti, since she had not troubled to ask after his health.

Shortly after this he wrote another letter to Akhnaton making various complaints, and stating that his messengers had been robbed in territory belonging to the Pharaoh, who must therefore make good their losses. A third letter makes similar complaints, and hints at future trouble. Meanwhile the King of Mitanni was on none too friendly terms with Akhnaton, and appears to have detained the Pharaoh's envoy, named Mani, thereby causing Akhnaton considerable anxiety. There was, in fact, a general tendency to disparage the Egyptian king, which must have been exceedingly galling to Akhnaton, who had the power to let loose upon Asia an army which would silence all insult, but did not find such a step consistent with his principles. In a letter which he wrote to one of the Syrian princes whose fidelity was doubtful, Akhnaton ends his despatch with the words: "I am very well, I the sun in the heavens, and my chariots and soldiers are exceedingly numerous; and from Upper Egypt even unto Lower Egypt, and from the place where the sun riseth even unto the place where he setteth, the whole country is in good cause and content." Thus we see that Akhnaton knew his power, and wished that others should know it; and it is therefore the more surprising that, as we shall presently find, he never chose to use it.

VII

THE LAST TWO YEARS OF THE REIGN OF AKHNATON

"I know, he said, what you like is to look at the mountains, or to go up among them and kill things. But I like the running water in a quiet garden, with a rose reflected in it, and the nightingale singing to it. Listen !"—MIRZA MAHOMED in "The Story of Valeh and Hadijeh."

I. THE HITTITE INVASION OF SYRIA

IN 1887 and 1891 the series of letters, now famous as the "Tell el Amarna Letters," were found by native diggers on the site of Akhnaton's city. They are tablets of baked clay inscribed in cuniform characters, and are the actual correspondence which passed between the Kings of Egypt, Babylon, Assyria, etc. From them the events about to be recorded have become known to us ; and the importance of the present excavations of the Egypt Exploration Society upon this site will be understood when it is realised that very probably more letters of this kind will be found.

The eastern end of the Mediterranean is bounded on the south by Egypt and the desert, on the east by Palestine and Syria, and on the north by Asia Minor, these roughly forming the three sides of a square. The conquests of the great warrior-Pharaoh Thutmosis III had carried the Egyptian power as far as the north-east corners of this formation—that is to say, to the point where Syria meets Asia Minor. The island of Cyprus is in shape not unlike a hand with index finger extended ; and this finger may be said to be pointing to the limit of Egyptian conquest, somewhere in the neighbourhood of the Amanus Mountains. The kingdom of Mitanni was situated on the banks of the Euphrates some distance inland from these mountains ; and as it acted as a buffer state between the Egyptian possessions in Syria and the unconquered lands beyond, the Pharaohs had taken care to unite themselves by marriage, as we have seen, with its rulers. Behind Mitanni to the north-east, the friendly kingdoms later known as Assyria marked the limits of the known world ; while to the north the hostile lands of Asia Minor lay in the possession of the Hittites, a warlike confederacy of peoples, perhaps the ancestors of the modern Armenians. From these hardy warriors the greatest danger to the Egyptian Empire in Syria was to be expected ; and the statesmen of Egypt must have cast many an anxious look towards those forbidding mountains which loomed beyond Mitanni. A southern movement of the Hittites, indications of which were already very apparent, would bring them swarming over and around the Amanus Mountains, either along the eastern and inland route through Mitanni, or along the western route beside the sea and over the Lebanon, or again, midway between these two routes, past the great cities of Tunip, Kadesh, and others, which stood to block the way.

When Akhnaton ascended the throne, Seplel was king of the Hittites, and was by way of being friendly to Egypt. Some of his people, however, crossed the frontiers of Mitanni and were repulsed by Dushratta, the king of that country. This caused some coldness between Seplel and the Pharaoh; and although the former sent an embassy to the City of the Horizon, the correspondence between the two monarchs presently ceased. The young idealist of Egypt seems to have held warfare in horror; and the Hittites were so essentially a fighting race that Akhnaton could have had no friendly feelings towards them. Soon we find that these Hittites, unable to overflow into the land of Mitanni, have moved along the eastern route and have seized the land of Amki, which lay on the sea-coast between the Amanus Mountains and the Lebanon. This movement might have been stopped by Aziru, an Amorite prince who ruled the territory between Amki and Mitanni, and whose duty, as an Egyptian vassal, was to check the southern incursions of the Hittites. But Aziru, like his father Abdashirta before him, was a man as ambitious as he was faithless, and his dealings both with the Hittites and with the Egyptians during the following years were unscrupulous in the extreme. It was his policy to play the one nation against the other, and to extend the scope of his own power at the expense of both.

2. AKHNATON'S CONSCIENTIOUS OBJECTIONS TO WARFARE

Akhnaton's policy in Syria, when considered from the point of view of an ordinary man, was of the weakest. Ideals cannot govern an empire won by the sword; and those who would apply the doctrine of " peace and goodwill " to turbulent subject races endanger the very principles which they would teach. While the young Pharaoh was chanting his psalms to the Aton in his growing capital, the princes of Syria were singing the revolutionary songs which presently were to ring in the ears of the isolated Egyptian garrisons. Little did they care for that tender Father of Mankind to whom Akhnaton's thin finger so earnestly pointed. They knew nothing of monotheism; they found no satisfaction in One who was the gentle ruler of all men without distinction of race. A true god to them was a vanquisher of other gods, a valiant leader in battle, a relentless avenger of insult. The furious Baal, the bloodthirsty Tishub, the terrible Ishtar—these were the deities that a man could love. How they scorned that God of Peace who was called the Only One! How they laughed at the young Pharaoh who had set aside the sword for the psalter, who hoped to rule his restless dominions by love alone!

Love! One stands amazed at the reckless idealism, the beautiful folly, of this Pharaoh who, in an age of turbulence, preached a religion of peace to seething Syria. Three thousand years later mankind is still blindly striving after these same ideals in vain. Nowadays one is familiar with the doctrine: a greater than Akhnaton has preached it, and has died for it. To-day God is known to us, and the peace of God is a thing hoped for; but at that far-off period, thirteen hundred years before the birth of Christ, two or three centuries before the age of David and Solomon, and many a year before the preaching of Moses, one is utterly surprised to behold the true light shining forth for a short moment like the sun through a rift in the clouds, and one knows that it has come too soon. Mankind, even now not ready, was then most wholly unprepared, and the price which Egypt paid for the ideals of her Pharaoh was no less than the complete loss of her dominions.

Akhnaton believed in God, and to him that belief meant a practical abhorrence of war. Marshalling the material available for the study of this period of history, one can interpret the events in Syria in only one way: Akhnaton definitely refused to do battle, believing that a resort to arms was an offence to God. Whether fortune or misfortune, gain or loss, was to be his lot, he would hold to his principles, and would not return to the old gods of battle.

It must be remembered that at this time the empire was the personal property of the Pharaoh, as every kingdom was of its king. Nobody ever considered a possession as belonging to the nation which had laid hands upon it, but only to that nation's king. It mattered very little to the Syrian peoples whether their owner was an Egyptian or a Syrian, though perhaps they preferred to be possessed by one of their own race. Akhnaton was thus doing his will with his own property. He was refusing to fight for his own possessions; he was acting literally upon the Christian principle of giving the cloak to him who had stolen the coat.

Patriotism was a sentiment unknown to the
world : devotion to the king's personal interest
was all that actuated loyalty in the subject, and
the monarch himself had but his own interests
to consider. Thus Akhnaton cannot be accused
of ruining his country by his refusal to go to war.
He was entitled to do what he liked with his
own personal property, and if he sacrificed his
possessions to his principles, the sacrifice was
made upon God's high altar, and the loss would
be felt by him alone. Such a loss, it is true,
would probably break his heart ; for he loved
Syria dearly, and he had had such great hopes
of uniting the empire by the tie of a common
religion. But for good or ill, he was determined
to stand aloof from the struggles upon which
Syria was now entering.

3. THE FAITHLESSNESS OF AZIRU

While Aziru, the Amorite, schemed on the
borders of Asia Minor, a Syrian prince named
Itakama suddenly set up an independent kingdom at Kadesh and joined hands with the
Hittites, thus cutting off the loyal city of Tunip.
the friendly kingdom of Mitanni, and the territory of the faithless Aziru, from direct intercourse with the Lebanon and Egypt's remaining
possessions in Palestine and Syria. Three loyal
vassal kings, perhaps assisted by Dushratta of

Mitanni, attacked the rebels, but were repulsed by Itakama and his Hittite allies.

Aziru at once turned the situation to his own advantage. Hemmed in between the Hittites on the north and this new kingdom of Kadesh on the south, he collected his armies and marched down the Orontes to the Mediterranean coast, capturing the cities near the mouth of that river and adding them to his possessions. Should the Hittites ask him to give an account of these proceedings, he could reply that he was, as it were, the advance-guard of the Hittite invasion of Syria, and was preparing the road for them. Should Itakama question him, he could say that he was, with friendly hands, linking the Hittites with Kadesh. And should Akhnaton call upon him for an explanation, he could answer that he was securing the land for the Egyptians against the Hittite advance.

No doubt Aziru preferred to keep his peace with the Hittites the most secure, for it was obvious that they were the rising people ; but at the same time he did not yet dare to show any hostility to Egypt, whose armies might at any moment be launched across the Mediterranean. Unable to hold a position of independence, he now thought it most prudent to allow the northmen to swarm southwards through his dominions, from Amki over and around the

Lebanon to Kadesh, where their ally Itakama dwelt. In return for this assistance he seems to have been allowed a free hand in the forwarding of his own interests, and we now find him turning his attention to the sea-coast cities of Simyra and Byblos, which nestled at the western foot of the Lebanon. Here, however, he received a check, and failed to obtain a footing. He therefore marched eastwards to the city of Niy, which he captured, slaying its king ; and both to the Hittites and to the Egyptians he seems to have pretended that he had taken this step in their interests.

On hearing of the fall of this city the governor of Tunip wrote a pathetic appeal to Akhnaton, asking for help ; for he was now quite isolated, and he knew that Aziru was a free-lance who cared not a jot for any but his own welfare.

" To the King of Egypt, my lord," runs the letter. " The inhabitants of Tunip, thy servant. May it be well with thee, and at the feet of our lord we fall. My lord, Tunip, thy servant, speaks, saying : Who formerly could have plundered Tunip without being plundered by Thutmosis III. ? The gods . . . of the King of Egypt, my lord, dwell in Tunip. May our lord ask his old men [if it be not so.] Now, however, we belong no more to our lord, the King of Egypt. . . . If his soldiers and chariots come too late, Aziru will make us like the city of Niy. If, however, we have to mourn, then the King of Egypt will mourn over these things which Aziru has done, for he will turn his hand against our lord. And when Aziru enters Simyra Aziru will do to us as he pleases, in the territory of our lord the King, and on account of these things our lord will have to lament. And now Tunip, thy city, weeps, and her tears are flowing and there is no help for us. For twenty years we have been sending to our lord the King, the King of Egypt, but there has not come to us a word—no, not one."

Several points become apparent from this letter. One sees that in the more distant cities of Syria the significance of Akhnaton's new religion was not understood. The governor of Tunip refers to the old gods of Egypt worshipped in that town, and he knows not, or cannot be brought to believe, that Akhnaton has become a monotheist. One sees that the memory of the terrible Thutmosis III and his victorious armies was still in men's minds, and was probably one of the main causes of the long-continued peace in Syria. Akhnaton's father, Amenophis III, had not concerned himself greatly with regard to his foreign dominions, and, as the people of Tunip had been asking for assistance for twenty years, it would seem that the danger which now beset them was already feared before that Pharaoh's death.

How, one asks, could Akhnaton read such a letter as this, and yet refuse to send a relieving army to Syria ? Byblos and Simyra were still loyally holding out ; and troops disembarked at

these ports could speedily be marched inland to
Tunip, could crush Itakama at Kadesh, and
could frighten Aziru into giving real assistance
to Dushratta and other loyal kings in holding
the Hittites back behind the Amanus Mountains. But this was Akhnaton's testing time;
and like that greater Teacher who, thirteen
hundred years later, was to preach the self-same
doctrine of personal sacrifice, one may suppose
that the Pharaoh suffered a very Agony as he
realised that his principles were leading him to
the loss of all his dearest possessions. His restless generals in Egypt, eager to march into Syria,
must have brought every argument to bear upon
him; but the boy would not now turn back.
" Put up thy sword into his place," he seems
to have said; " for all they that take the sword
shall perish with the sword."

4. THE FIGHTING IN SYRIA BECOMES GENERAL

At this time the King of Byblos was one
named Ribaddi, a fine old soldier who was loyal
to Egypt in his every thought and deed. He
wrote to Akhnaton urging him to send troops
to relieve the garrison of Simyra, upon which
Aziru was again pressing close; for if Simyra
fell, he knew that Byblos could not for long
hold out. Presently we find that Zimrida, the
king of the neighbouring port of Sidon, has

opened his gates to Aziru, and has marched with him against Tyre. Abimilki, the King of Tyre, at once wrote to Akhnaton asking for assistance ; but on receiving no reply he, too, appears to have thrown in his lot with Aziru. Ribaddi was now quite isolated at Byblos ; and from the beleaguered city he wrote to the Pharaoh telling him that "Simyra is like a bird in a snare." Akhnaton made no reply ; and in a short time Ribaddi wrote again, saying, "Simyra, your fortress, is now in the power of the Khabiri."

These Khabiri were the Beduin from behind Palestine, who were being used as mercenaries by Aziru, and who themselves were making small conquests in the south on their own behalf. Thus the southern cities of Megiddo, Askalon, Gezer, and others, write to the Pharaoh asking for aid against them. Exasperated, however, by Akhnaton's inaction, Askalon and Gezer, together with the city of Lachish, threw off the Egyptian yoke and attacked Jerusalem, which was still loyal to Egypt, being held by an officer named Abdkhiba. This loyal soldier at once sent a despatch to Akhnaton, part of which read as follows :—

> The King's whole land, which has begun hostilities with me, will be lost. Behold the territory of Seir, as far as Carmel, its princes are wholly lost ; and hostility prevails against me. . . . As long as ships were upon the sea the strong arm of the King occupied

Naharin and Kash, but now the Khabiri are occupying
the King's cities.   There remains not one prince to
my lord, the King ; every one is ruined. . . .   Let
the King take care of his land, and . . . let him send
troops. . . .   For if no troops come in this year, the
whole territory of my lord the King will perish. . . .
If there are no troops in this year, let the King send his
officer to fetch me and my brothers, that we may die
with our lord, the King.

To this letter the writer added a postscript
addressed to Akhnaton's secretary, with whom
he was evidently acquainted. " Bring these words
plainly before my lord the King," runs this
pathetic appeal. " The whole land of my lord,
the King, is going to ruin."

The letters sent to Akhnaton from the few
princes who remained loyal form a collection
which even now moves the reader. To Akhnaton
they must have been so many sword-thrusts,
and one may picture him praying passionately
for strength to set them aside. Soon it would
seem that the secretaries hardly troubled to show
them to him ; and ultimately they were so effect-
ually pigeon-holed that they have only recently
been discovered. The Pharaoh permitted himself
to answer some of them, and seems to have
asked questions as to the state of affairs ; but
never does he offer any encouragement. Lapaya,
one of the princes of the south, who had evidently received a communication from Akhnaton

o

in which his fidelity was questioned, wrote saying that if the Pharaoh ordered him to drive a
sword of bronze into his heart he would do so.
It is a commentary upon the veracity of the
Oriental that in subsequent letters this prince is
stated to have attacked Megiddo, and ultimately
to have been slain while fighting against the
Egyptian loyalists.

Addudaian, a king of some unknown city of
south Judea, acknowledges the receipt of a letter
from Akhnaton in which he was asked to remain
loyal; and he complains, in reply, of the loss of
various possessions. Dagantakala, the king of
another city, writes imploring the Pharaoh to
rescue him from the Khabiri. Ninur, a queen
of a part of Judea, who calls herself Akhnaton's
handmaid, entreats the Pharaoh to save her,
and records the capture of one of her cities by
the Khabiri.

And so the letters run on, each telling of some
disaster to the Egyptian cause, and each voicing
the bitter complaint of those who were being
sacrificed to the principles of a king who had
grasped the meaning of civilisation too soon.

5. AZIRU AND RIBADDI FIGHT TO A FINISH

Meanwhile Ribaddi was holding Byblos vali-
antly against Aziru's armies, and many were the
despatches which he sent to Akhnaton asking

for assistance against Aziru.   Nothing could have
been easier than the despatch of a few hundred
men across the Mediterranean to the beleaguered
port, and the number which Ribaddi asks for is
absurdly small. Akhnaton, however, would not
send a single man, but instead wrote a letter
of gentle rebuke to Aziru, telling him to come to
the City of the Horizon to explain his conduct.
Aziru wrote at once to one of Akhnaton's
courtiers, who was his friend, telling him to
speak to the Pharaoh and to set matters right.

He explained that he could not leave Syria at
that time, for he must remain to defend Tunip
against the Hittites. The reader, who has seen
the letter written by the governor of Tunip
asking for help against Aziru, will realise the
perfidy of this Amorite, who was now, no doubt,
preparing to capture Tunip for the sake of its
riches, and, having done so, would tell Akhnaton
that he had entered it to hold it against the
Hittites.

Akhnaton then wrote to Aziru insisting that
he should rebuild the city of Simyra, which he
had destroyed ; but Aziru again replied that he
was too busy in defending Egyptian interests
against the inroads of the Hittites to give his
attention to this matter for at least a year. To
this Akhnaton sent a mild reply ; but Aziru,
fearing that the letter might contain some

matter which it would be better for him not to hear, contrived to evade the messenger, and the despatch was brought back to Egypt. He wrote to the Pharaoh, however, saying that he would see to it that the cities captured by him should continue to pay tribute as usual to Egypt.

The tribute seems to have reached the City of the Horizon in correct manner until the last years of the reign,[1] though probably it was much less in quantity than had been customary. There was general confusion in Syria, as we have seen ; but, as in the case of the struggle between Aziru and Ribaddi, where both professed their loyalty to Egypt, so, in all the chaos, there was a make-believe fidelity to the Pharaoh. The tribute was thus paid each year by a large number of cities, and it was probably not till the seventeenth and last year of Akhnaton's reign that this pretence of loyalty was altogether discarded.

In desperate straits at Byblos, Ribaddi made a perilous journey to the neighbouring city of Beyrût in order to attempt to collect reinforcements. No sooner had he left, however, than an insurrection occurred at Byblos, and Ribaddi

[1] The reception of the tribute recorded in the tomb of Meryra II. (see page 148), although dated in the twelfth year of the reign, may represent a later event, since six daughters are shown in the scene ; and it is not likely that the sixth daughter was born before the fifteenth year. Perhaps the date is a misreading or miswriting, influenced by that given in the tomb of Huya.

paid for his loyalty to Egypt by losing the support of his own subjects. Presently Beyrût surrendered to Aziru, and Ribaddi was forced to fly. After many an adventure the stout old king managed to regain control of Byblos, and to set about the further defence of the city.

Meanwhile Aziru had paid a rapid visit to Egypt, partly to justify his conduct and partly, no doubt, to ascertain the condition of affairs on the Nile. With Oriental cunning he managed to satisfy Akhnaton that his intentions were not hostile to Egypt, and so returned to the Lebanon. Ribaddi, hearing of this, at once sent his son to the City of the Horizon to expose Aziru's perfidy and to plead for assistance against him. At the same time he wrote to Akhnaton a pathetic account of his misfortunes. Four members of his family had been taken prisoners ; his brother was constantly conspiring against him ; old age and disease pressed heavily upon him. All his possessions had been taken from him, all his lands devastated ; he had been reduced by famine and the privations of a long siege to a state of utter destitution, and he could not much longer hold out. " The gods of Byblos," he writes, " are angry with me and sore displeased ; for I have sinned against the gods, and therefore I do not come before my lord the King." Was his sin, one wonders, the adoption for a while of Akhnaton's faith ? To this communication Akhnaton seems to have made no reply.

6. AKHNATON CONTINUES TO REFUSE TO SEND HELP

The messengers who arrived at the City of the Horizon of Aton, dusty and travel-stained, to deliver the many letters asking for help, must have despaired indeed when they observed the manner in which the news was received. Hateful to these hardy soldiers of the empire were the fine quays at which their galleys moored ; hateful the fair villas and shaded avenues of the city ; and thrice hateful the rolling hymns to the Aton which came to them from the temple halls as they hurried to the Pharaoh's palace. The townspeople smiled at their haste in this city of dreams ; the court officials delayed the delivery of their letters, scoffing at the idea of urgency in the affairs of Asia ; and finally these wretched documents, written—if ever letters were so written—with blood and with tears, were pigeon-holed in the city archives and utterly forgotten save by Akhnaton himself. Instead of the brave music of the drums and bugles of the relieving army which these messengers had hoped to muster, there rang in their maddened ears only the

ceaseless chants of the priestly ceremonies and
the pattering love-songs of private festivals.
Newly come from the sweat and the labour of
the road, their brains still racked with the
horror of war and yet burning with the vast
hopes of empire, they looked with scorn at the
luxury of Egypt's new capital, and heard with
disgust the dainty tales of the flowers. The
lean, sad-eyed Pharaoh, with his crooked head
and his stooping shoulders, would speak only
of his God; and, clad in simple clothes un-
relieved by a single jewel, there was nothing
martial in his appearance to give them hope.
From the beleaguered cities which they had so
lately left there came to them the bitter cry
for succour; and it was not possible to drown
that cry in words of peace, nor in the jangle of
the systrum or the warbling of the pipes. Who,
thought the waiting messengers, could resist
that piteous call: " Thy city weeps, and her
tears are flowing " ? Who could sit idle in the
City of the Horizon when the proud empire, won
with the blood of the noblest soldiers of the
great Thutmosis, was breaking up before their
eyes ? What mattered all the philosophies in
the world, and all the gods in heaven, when
Egypt's great dominions were being wrested from
her ? The splendid Lebanon, the white kingdoms
of the sea, Askalon and Ashdod, Tyre and Sidon,

Simyra and Byblos, the hills of Jerusalem, Kadesh
and the great Orontes, the fair Jordan, Tunip,
Aleppo, the distant Euphrates. . . . What
counted a creed against these ? God ? The truth ?
The only god was He of the Battles, who had led
Egypt into Syria ; the only truth the doctrine
of the sword, which had held her there for so
many years.

Looking back across these thirty-two centuries,
can one yet say whether the Pharaoh was in the
right, or whether his soldiers were the better
minded ? On the one hand there is culture,
refinement, love, thought, prayer, goodwill, and
peace ; on the other hand, power, might, health,
hardihood, bravery, and struggle. One knows
that Akhnaton's theories were the more civilised, the more ideal ; but is there not a pulse
which stirs in sympathy with those who were
holding the citadels of Asia ? We can give our
approval to the ideals of the young king, but
we cannot see his empire fall without bitterly
blaming him for the disaster. Yet in passing
judgment, in calling the boy to account for the
loss of Syria, there is the consciousness that
above our tribunal sits a judge to whom war
must assuredly be abhorrent, and in whose
eyes the struggle of the nations must utterly
lack its drama. Thus, even now, Akhnaton
eludes our criticism, and but raises once more

that eternal question which as yet has no answer.

7. AKHNATON'S HEALTH GIVES WAY

Perhaps in order to create an impression, he now celebrated his jubilee festival, as is indicated on an inscribed fragment of stone, now at Oxford. The jubilee ceremony was usually held thirty years after a king had been nominated to the throne ; and Akhnaton, being now thirty years of age, and regarding his nomination as dating from the hour of his birth, did not longer delay the festivities.

It is possible that the Pharaoh now realised his position, and one may suppose that he tried as best he could to pacify the turbulent princes by all the arts of diplomacy. It does not seem, however, that he yet fully appreciated the catastrophe which was now almost inevitable—the complete loss of Syria. He could not bring himself to believe that the princes of that country would play him false ; and he could have had no idea that he was being so entirely fooled by such men as Aziru. But when at last the tribute ceased to come in regularly, then, too late, he knew that disaster was upon him.

The thoughts which now must have held sway in his mind could not have failed to carry him down the dark steps of depression to the very

pit of despair, and one may picture him daily
cast prone upon the floor before the high altar
of the Aton, and nightly tossing sleepless upon
his royal bed. It seems that he had placed
great reliance upon a certain official, named
Bikhuru, who was acting as Egyptian commis-
sioner in Palestine ; but now it is probable
that he received news of that unfortunate personage's flight, and later of his murder.[1] Then
came the report that Byblos had fallen, and one
is led to suppose that that truly noble soldier
Ribaddi did not survive the fall of the city
which he had so tenaciously held. The news
of the surrender of other important Egyptian
strongholds followed rapidly, and still there
came the pathetic appeal for help from the
minor posts which yet held out.

Akhnaton was now just thirty years of age,
and already the cares of the whole world seemed
to rest upon his shoulders. Lean and lank was
his body ; his face was thin and lined with
worry ; and in his eye one might, perhaps, have
seen that hunted look which comes to those
who are dogged by disaster. It is probable that
he now suffered acutely from the distressing
malady to which he was a victim, and there
must have been times when he felt himself
upon the verge of madness. His misshapen

[1] Breasted : History, p. 388.

skull came nigh to bursting with the full thoughts
of his aching brain, and the sad knowledge that
he had failed must have pressed upon his mind
like some unrelenting finger. The invocations
to the Aton which rang in his head made confusion with the cry of Syria. Now he listened
to the voices of his choirs lauding the sweetness
of life; and now, breaking in upon the chant,
did he not hear the solemn voices of his fathers
calling to him from the Hills of the West to give
account of his stewardship? Could he then
find solace in trees and in flowers? Could he cry
"Peace" when there was red tumult in his brain?
His moods at this time must have given cause
for the greatest alarm, and his behaviour was,
no doubt, sufficiently erratic to render even
those nobles who had so blindly followed him
mistrustful of their leader. In a frenzy of zeal
in the adoration of the Aton, Akhnaton now
gave orders that the name of all other gods should
suffer the same fate as that of Amon, and should
be erased from every inscription throughout
the land. This order was never fully carried
out; but one may still see in the temples of
Karnak, Medinet Habu, and elsewhere, and upon
many lesser monuments, the chisel marks which
have partially blurred out the names of Ptah,
Hathor, and other deities, and have obliterated
the offending word "gods."

The consternation which this action must have caused was almost sufficient to bring about a revolution in the provinces, where the old gods were still dearly loved by the people. The erasing of the name of Amon had been, after all, a direct war upon a certain priesthood, and did not very materially affect any other localities than that of Thebes. But the suppression of the numerous priesthoods of the many deities who held sway throughout Egypt threw into disorder the whole country, and struck at the heart not of one but of a hundred cities. Was the kindly old artificer Ptah, with his hammer and his chisel, to be tumbled into empty space? Was the beautiful, the gracious Hathor—the Venus of the Nile—to be thrown down from her celestial seat? Was it possible to banish Khnum, the goat-headed potter who lived in the caves of the Cataract, from the life of the city of Elephantine; the mysterious jackal Wepwat from the hearts of the men of Abydos; or the ancient crocodile Sebek from the ships and the fields of Ombos? Every town had its local god, and every god its priesthood; and surely the Pharaoh was mad who attempted to make war upon these legions of heaven. This Aton, whom the king called upon them to worship, was so remote, so infinitely above their heads. Aton did not sit with them at their hearth-side to watch the

kettle boil; Aton did not play a sweet-toned
flute amongst the reeds of the river; Aton did
not bring a fairy gift to the new-born babe.
Where was the sacred tree in whose branches
one might hope to see him seated?—where
was the eddy of the Nile in which he loved to
bathe?—and where was the rock at whose foot
one might place, as a fond offering, a bowl of
milk? The people loved their old gods, whose
simple ways, kind hearts, and quick tempers
made them understandable to mortal minds.
But a god who reigned alone in solitary isolation,
who, more remote even than the Jehovah of the
Hebrews, rode not upon the clouds nor moved
upon the wings of the wind, was hardly a deity
to whom they could open their hearts. True,
the sunrise and the sunset were the visible signs
of the godhead; but let the reader ask any
modern Egyptian peasant whether there is aught
to stir the pulses in these two great phenomena,
and he will realise that the glory of the skies
could not have appealed particularly to the lesser
subjects of Akhnaton, who, moreover, were not
permitted to bow the knee to the flaming orb
itself. When the Christian religion took hold of
these peasants, and presented for their acceptance
the same idea of a remote though loving and
considerate God, it was only by the elevation of
saints and devils, angels and powers of darkness,

almost to the rank of demigods, that the faith prospered. But Akhnaton allowed no such tampering with the primary doctrine, and St. George and all the saints would have suffered the erasure of their very names.

8. AKHNATON'S LAST DAYS AND DEATH

The troubles which Akhnaton by such actions gathered around himself, while disturbing to his adherents, must have given some degree of pleasure to those nobles who saw in the king's downfall the only hope of Egypt. Horemheb, the commander-in-chief of the inactive armies could now begin to prepare himself against the time when he should lead a force into Syria to restore Egyptian prestige. Tutankhaton, betrothed to Akhnaton's third daughter, could dream of the days when he would make himself Pharaoh, and carry the court back to glorious Thebes. Even Meryra, the High Priest of Aton, seems to have allowed his thoughts to drift away from the City of the Horizon wherein the sun of Egypt's glory had set, for it does not seem that he ever made use of the tomb there prepared for him. These last stages of Akhnaton's life must thus have been embittered by a doubt of the sincerity of his closest friends, and by the knowledge that, in spite of all their protestations, he had failed to plant "the truth" in their hearts.

The queen had borne him no son to succeed to the throne, and there appeared to be nobody to whom he could impart what he felt to be his last instructions. There can be no question that he was still greatly loved by those who surrounded his person, but there were few who hoped that his religion, so disastrous to Egypt, would survive him. In this extremity Akhnaton turned to a certain noble, probably not of royal blood, whose name seems to have been Smenkhkara, though some have read it Saakara.[1] Nothing is known regarding his previous career, but one may suppose that he appeared to Akhnaton to be the least unreliable of his followers. To him the king imparted his instructions, revealing all that words could draw from his teeming brain. The little Princess Merytaton, now but twelve years of age, was called from her games, and with pomp and ceremony was married to this Smenkhkara, thus making him the legitimate heir to the throne, Merytaton being the eldest daughter and sole heiress of the Pharaoh.

There is a little portrait head of a queen now in Berlin, which was found in the Fayoum and which perhaps represents Merytaton, since it is quite unlike the known heads of Queens Tiy

[1] It is doubtful whether the second sign is *menkh* or *aa*, they being somewhat alike.

and Nefertiti, and yet, by the style of the art, evidently belongs to the reign of Akhnaton.

Feeling that his days were numbered, Akhnaton then associated Smenkhkara upon the throne with him as co-ruler, and was thus able to familiarise the people with their future lord. In later years, after Akhnaton's death, Smenkhkara was wont to write after his name the words "beloved of Akhnaton," as though to indicate that his claim to the throne was due to Akhnaton's affection for him, as well as to the rights derived from his wife.

But what mattered the securing of the succession to the throne when that throne had been shaken to its very foundations, and now seemed to be upon the verge of utter wreck? Akhnaton could no longer stave off the impending crash, and from all sides there gathered the forces which were to overwhelm him. His government was chaotic. The plotting and scheming of the priests of Amon showed signs of coming to a successful issue. The anger of the priesthoods of the other gods of Egypt hung over the palace like some menacing stormcloud. The soldiers, eager to march upon Syria as in the days of the great Thutmosis III, chafed at their enforced idleness, and watched with increasing restlessness the wreck of the empire.

Now through the streets of the city there

passed the weary messengers of Asia hurrying to the palace, no longer bearing the appeals of kings and generals for support, but announcing the fall of the last cities of Syria and the slaughter of the last left of their rulers. The scattered remnants of the garrisons staggered back to the Nile at the heels of these messengers, pursued to the very frontiers of Egypt by the triumphant Asiatics. From the north the Hittites poured into Syria; from the south the Khabiri swarmed over the land. As the curtain is rung down on the turbulent scene, one catches a glimpse of the wily Aziru, his hands still stained with the blood of Ribaddi and of many another loyal prince, snatching at this city and trampling on that. At last he has cast aside his mask, and with the tribute which had been promised to Egypt he now, no doubt, placates the ascending Hittites, whose suzerainty alone he admits.

The tribute having ceased, the Egyptian treasury soon stood empty, for the government of the country was too confused to permit of the proper gathering of the taxes, and the working of the gold-mines could not be organised. Much had been expended on the building of the City of the Horizon, and now the king knew not where to turn for money. In the space of a few years Egypt had been reduced from a world power

R

to the position of a petty state, from the richest country known to man to the humiliating condition of a bankrupt kingdom.

Surely one may picture Akhnaton now in his last hours, his jaw fallen, his sunken eyes widely staring, as the full realisation of the utter failure of all his hopes came to him. He had sacrificed Syria to his principles; but the sacrifice was of no avail, since his doctrines had not taken root even in Egypt. He knew now that the religion of the Aton would not outlive him, that the knowledge of the love of God was not yet to be made known to the world. Even at this moment the psalms of the Aton were beating upon his ears, the hymns to the God who had forsaken him were drifting into his palace with the scent of the flowers; and the birds which he loved were singing as merrily in the luxuriant gardens as ever they sang when they had inspired a line in the king's great poem. But upon him now there had fallen the blackness of despair, and already the darkness of coming death was closing around him. The misery of failure must have ground him down as beneath the very mountains of the west themselves, and the weight of the knowledge of all that he had lost could not be borne by his enfeebled frame.

History tells us only that, simultaneously with

the fall of his empire, Akhnaton died ; and the doctors who have examined his body report that death may well have been due to some form of stroke or fit. But in the imagination there seems to ring across the years a cry of complete despair, and one can picture the emaciated figure of this " beautiful child of the Aton " fall forward upon the painted palace-floor and lie still amidst the red poppies and the dainty butterflies there depicted.

VIII

THE FALL OF THE RELIGION OF AKHNATON

" Thus disappeared the most remarkable figure in early Oriental history. . . . There died with him such a spirit as the world had never seen before."—BREASTED : " History of Egypt."

---

1. THE BURIAL OF AKHNATON

THE body of Akhnaton was embalmed in the city which he had founded; and while these mortal parts of the great idealist were undergoing the lengthy process of mummification, the new Pharaoh Smenkhkara made a feeble attempt to retain the spirit of his predecessor in the new *régime*. Practically nothing is known of his brief reign, but it is apparent from subsequent events that he entirely failed to carry on the work of Akhnaton, and the period of his sovereignty is marked by a general tendency to abandon the religion of the Aton. Smenkhkara had dated the first year of his reign from the day of his accession as co-ruler with Akhnaton, and thus it is that there are no inscriptions

found which record his first year, although there
are many references to his second year. The
main event must have occurred some three
months after the commencement of his sole
reign, when the body of Akhnaton was carried
in solemn state through the streets of the city
and across the desert to the tomb which had
been made for him in the distant cliffs.

The mummy had been wrapped, as was usual,
in endless strips of linen ; and amongst these
there was placed upon the royal throat a necklace of gold, and over the face or breast an ornament cut in flat gold foil representing a vulture
with wings outstretched—a Pharaonic symbol
of divine protection. In many burials of this
dynasty a vulture such as this was placed upon
the mummy ; and representations of an exactly
similar ornament are shown in the tombs of
Sennefer, Horemheb, and others at Thebes. It
is somewhat surprising that the body of Akhnaton, who was so averse to all old customs,
should thus have this royal talisman upon it ;
and it would seem that some of the strict rules of
the Aton worshipper had already been relaxed
by his successor. Akhnaton had retained but
few of the ancient divine symbols, so far as
one can tell from the reliefs and paintings—
for instance, the uræus or cobra, the sphinx, and
the hawk, which were often used as ornaments.

But one may ask whether the vulture had really been dispensed with by him. It is true that he banned the vulture-hieroglyph in the inscriptions, as we have already seen on the outer coffin of Queen Tiy ;[1] but his reason for so doing was that by such a hieroglyph the name of the goddess Mut was called to mind, and that goddess, being the consort of Amon, was not to be tolerated. The vulture which was laid upon the mummy, however, had nothing to do with Mut, nor had it any likeness to the hieroglyph. It was originally a representation of the presiding genius of Upper Egypt, and corresponded to the uræus, which primarily represented the power of Lower Egypt. It is true, again, that it was the custom for the Pharaohs to be shown in the sculptures and paintings with this vulture hovering in protection over their heads, and that Akhnaton seems to have dispensed with such a symbol. But this was perhaps due to the fact that the disk and rays, symbolic of Aton, had taken its place above the royal figure. There is no reason, after all, to suppose that this form of vulture was absolutely banned, since the uræus and the hawk were retained ;[2] and though, as will

[1] Page 162.

[2] The scarab, another symbol from older times, seems to have been retained, for a gold heart-scarab is said to have been found in Akhnaton's tomb.—Petrie : History of Egypt, ii. 220.

presently be seen, it will be natural to think that it was placed on Akhnaton's mummy at his successor's suggestion, there is nothing to show that Akhnaton himself did not desire it to be laid there.

Over the linen bandages on the body there were placed ribbons of gold foil encircling the mummy—probably around the shoulders, the middle, and the knees—joined to other ribbons running the length of the body at the back and front. These ribbons were inscribed with Akhnaton's name and titles, and thus recorded for all time the identity of the mummy to which they adhered. Money being found somehow, the body was wrapped in sheets of pure gold, sufficiently thin to be flexible, and was placed in a splendid coffin, designed in the usual form of a recumbent figure, and inlaid in a dazzling manner with rare stones and coloured glass, the face being carved in wood and covered with stout gold foil. Down the front of this coffin ran a simple inscription, the hieroglyphs of which were also inlaid. It read: "The beautiful Prince, The Chosen One of Ra, the King of Upper and Lower Egypt, living in Truth, Lord of the Two Lands, Akhnaton, the beautiful child of the living Aton, whose name shall live for ever and ever." There is one curious feature about this inscription. When Akhnaton made the outer coffin for his mother, in or about the twelfth year of his reign, he was particularly careful not to use the hieroglyph representing the goddess Maat when writing the word *maat*, " truth." But this sign is employed upon his own coffin ; and one can only presume therefore, that the coffin was made some years before his death. The appearance of the earlier form of the name of the Aton on a necklace ornament and on a piece of gold foil found with the body is an indication that these objects were also made in the middle of the reign.

Below the feet of the coffin a short prayer was inscribed, which, as will presently be remarked, was probably composed by the king himself, and in which he addressed himself to the Aton.

The royal mummy was now carried to its tomb and there deposited, together with such funeral furniture and offerings as were considered neces- sary. The four alabaster canopic jars, always conspicuous in an Egyptian burial, were here not wanting. The stopper of each jar was exquisitely carved to represent the head of Akhnaton, wearing the usual male wig of the period, and having the royal cobra upon the forehead. These heads seem by their style to date from early in the king's reign ; and one may assume that they were made several years previous to his death, so as to be ready whenever that event might occur. Every Pharaoh caused his tomb to be made during his lifetime, and there is no reason to suppose that the coffin and burial equipment were not also prepared in readiness.

2. THE COURT RETURNS TO THEBES

For some time the court remained loyal to the memory of Akhnaton, and Smenkhkara's right to the throne was recognised as being based upon the two facts that he was the " beloved of Akhnaton " and that he was the husband of Akhnaton's eldest daughter, Merytaton. The recent excavations of the Egypt Exploration Society have shown that in one of the small temples in the city the name of the now dowager queen Nefertiti has been erased here and there, and that of Merytaton substituted, though Akhnaton's name has not been altered. This suggests that Smenkhkara, recognising the above-mentioned bases of his claim to the throne, was now pushing his wife, Akhnaton's daughter, into prominence and was beginning to ignore Nefertiti. History does not tell us what was the final fate of Nefertiti, but since nothing more is heard of her it is to be supposed that she soon died. Perhaps the Egypt Exploration Society's excavations will reveal to us something of her end, which, it would seem, must have been very sorrowful.

Smenkhkara died, or was deposed, about a year after Akhnaton's death. He was succeeded by another noble, Tutankhaton,[1] who obtained in marriage Akhnaton's second daughter Ankh-senpaaton, a girl barely twelve years old. Thus Smenkhkara's wife, Merytaton, became a dowager-queen at the age of thirteen or so, and her little sister took her place upon the throne.

By this time the priests of Amon had begun to hold up their heads once more, and to scheme for the downfall of Aton with renewed energy. Pressure was soon brought to bear on Tutankh-aton, and he had not been upon the throne more than a year or so when he was persuaded to consider the abandonment of the City of the Horizon and his return to Thebes. He did not yet turn entirely from the religion of the Aton, but attempted to take a middle course between the two factions, giving full licence both to the worshippers of the Aton and to those of Amon. Horemheb, the commander-in-chief of the idle army, seems to have been one of the leaders of the reactionary movement. He did not concern himself so much with the

---

[1] Probably he is to be identified with Tutu, a well-known noble of this period—the words *ankhaton*, " Living in Aton," being added to make the name more majestic.

religious aspect of the question : there was as much to be said on the one side as on the other. But it was he who knocked at the doors of the heart of Egypt and urged the nation to awake to the danger in Asia. For him there were no scruples as to warfare, and the doctrine of the sword found favour in his sight. An expedition was fitted out, and the reigning Pharaoh was persuaded to lead it. Thus we read that Horemheb was " the companion of his Lord upon the battle-field on that day of the slaying of the Asiatics."[1] Akhnaton had dreamed of the universal peace which still is a far-off wraith to man-kind ; but Horemheb was a practical man in whom that dream would have been but weakness which was such mighty strength in the dead King.

The new Pharaoh now changed his name from Tutankhaton to Tutankhamon, and, to the sound of martial music, returned to Thebes.

The abandonment of the City of the Horizon appears to have been carried out in haste, and one may perhaps suppose that events so shaped

[1] See note on page 58. This inscription is found on the doorpost of the tomb of Horemheb, which, by the greatly increased titles, were set up some time after the rest of the tomb was finished and thus probably in the reign of Tutankhaton. A fragment of gold-leaf has been found showing this king in his chariot charging Asiatic enemies. The present writer found part of a shrine of his in the desert on the road to the gold mines. See "Travels in the Upper Egyptian Deserts" (Blackwood).

themselves as to place in the hands of the reactionary party the power to demand a sudden
and instant evacuation of Akhnaton's city. The
excavations of the Egypt Exploration Society
have revealed the bones of Akhnaton's dogs
in the royal kennels, as though these unfortunate
animals had been left there to starve when the
court marched away ; and dead oxen have also
been found in the sheds of the King's farm,
lying where they were abandoned. The city
itself shows other signs of having been suddenly
left to its fate, and it was not long before the
palaces and the villas became the home of the
jackals and the owls, while the temples were
partly pulled down to provide stone for other
works.

The sands of the desert soon buried the
ruins, and the excavations now in progress are
revealing the forsaken houses and gardens in
a marvellous state of preservation.

However much the reigning Pharaoh differed
in views from Akhnaton, it would not have
been possible to leave the royal body lying in
sight of this wreck of all the hopes that had
been his. Akhnaton, moreover, was Tutankhamon's father-in-law, and it was only through
the rights of Akhnaton's daughter that the
Pharaoh held the throne. His memory was
still regarded with reverence by many of his late

followers, and there could be no question of leaving his body in the deserted city. It was therefore carried to Thebes in its coffin, together with the four canopic jars, and was placed, for want of a proper sepulchre, in the tomb of Queen Tiy, which had been reopened for the purpose.

Tutankhamon showed the trend of his policy by both restoring the temple of the Aton at Karnak and at the same time repairing the damage done by Akhnaton to the works of Amon. An inscription from his reign says that he found the temples of all the gods and goddesses desolate from end to end of the country, and that he restored them and revived the worship in them. The style of art which he favoured was a modified form of Akhnaton's method, and the influence of his movement is still apparent in the new king's work. He did not reign long enough, however, to display much originality, and after a few years he disappears, almost unnoticed, from the stage. On his death the question of inviting Horemheb to fill the vacant throne must have been seriously considered, but there was another candidate in the field. This was Akhnaton's father-in-law, Ay, who had been one of the most important nobles in the group of courtiers at the City of the Horizon, and who, as the father of Queen

Nefertiti, was the only remaining male member of Akhnaton's family. He had been loudest in the praises of the preacher king and of his doctrines, and he still retained the title " Father-in-law of the King " as his most cherished designation.

Religious feeling at this time was running high, for the partisans of Amon and those of Aton seem still to have been struggling for the supremacy, and Ay appeared to have been regarded as the most likely man to bridge the gulf between the two factions. A favourite of Akhnaton, and still tolerant of all that was connected with the late movement, he was not averse to the cult of Amon, and by conciliating both parties he managed to obtain the throne for himself. His power, however, did not last for long, and as the priests of Amon regained the confidence of the nation at the expense of the worshippers of the Aton, so the prestige of Ay declined. His past relationship to Akhnaton, which even as king he carefully recorded within his cartouche, now told against him rather than for him, and about eight years after the death of Akhnaton he disappeared like his predecessors.

3. THE REIGN OF HOREMHEB

There was now no question who should succeed. All eyes were turned to Horemheb, who had already almost as much power as the Pharaoh. The commander-in-chief at once ascended the throne, and was received by the populace with the utmost rejoicings. At this time there was living at Thebes the Princess Nezemmut, the sister[1] of Akhnaton's Queen Nefertiti, and daughter of King Ay. Nezemmut had perhaps married some Egyptian nobleman, but was now a widow, and had recently been appointed to the post of " Divine Consort,"—that is to say, High Priestess—of Amon. As she was probably the younger sister of Nefertiti, she may have been about six or eight years of age when Nefertiti was married to Akhnaton. Hence she would have been about twenty-three or so at his death, and would now be somewhat over thirty.

To this princess, as daughter and heiress of the last king, Ay, and as representing the priesthood of Amon, and also as not having the now condemning blood relationship to Akhnaton which debarred any of the " heretic's " daughters who may still have been alive, Horemheb was at once married, for the purpose of legitimising his accession. The religion of the Aton was now fast disappearing. In a tomb dating from the third year of Horemheb's reign, the words " Ra whose body is Aton " occur; but this is

---

[1] She is shown as Nefertiti's sister in the tomb of Ay at Tel el Amarna.

the last mention of the Aton, and henceforth Amon-Ra is unquestionably supreme. A certain Paatonemheb, who had been one of Akhnaton's favourites, was at about this time appointed High Priest of Ra-Horakhti at Heliopolis, and thus the last traces of the religion of the Aton were merged into the Heliopolitan theology, from which that religion at the beginning had emanated.

The neglected shrines of the old gods once more echoed with the chants of the priests throughout the whole land of Egypt. Inscriptions tell us that Horemheb " restored the temples from the pools of the Delta marshes to Nubia. He fashioned a hundred images . . . with all splendid and costly stones. He established for them daily offerings every day. All the vessels of their temples were wrought of silver and gold. He equipped them with priests and with ritual priests, and with the choicest of the army. He transferred to them lands and cattle, supplied with all necessary equipment." By these gifts to the neglected gods Horemheb was striving to bring Egypt back to its natural condition; and with a strong hand he was guiding the country from chaos to order, from fantastic Utopia to the solid old Egypt of the past. He was, in fact, the very apostle of the Normal.

He led his armies into the Sudan, and returned with a procession of captive chieftains roped before him. He had none of Akhnaton's qualms regarding human suffering, and these unfortunate prisoners are seen to have their arms bound in the most cruel manner. Finding the country to be lawless he drafted a number of stern laws, and with sound justice administered his kingdom. Knowing that Syria could not long remain quiet, he organised the Egyptian troops, and so prepared them that, but a few years after his death, the soldiers of the reigning Pharaoh were swarming once more over the lands which Akhnaton had lost.

4. THE PERSECUTION OF AKHNATON'S MEMORY

The priests of Amon-Ra had now begun openly to denounce Akhnaton as a villian and a heretic, and as they restored the name of their god where it had been erased, so they hammered out the name and figure of Akhnaton wherever they saw it. Presently they pulled down the Aton temple at Karnak, and used the blocks of stone in the building of a pylon for Amon-Ra. Soon it was felt that Akhnaton's body could no longer lie in state, together with that of Queen Tiy, in the Valley of the Tombs of the Kings. The sepulchre was therefore opened

s

once more and the name " Akhnaton " was everywhere erased from the inscriptions, as was his
figure from the scenes upon the shrine of Queen
Tiy. The mummy was lifted from its coffin and
the royal name was cut out of the gold ribbons
which passed round it, both at the back and
the front. It was then replaced in the coffin,
and from this the name was also erased.

The question may be asked why it was that
the body was not torn to pieces and scattered
to the four winds, since the king was now so
fiercely hated. The Egyptians, however, entertained a peculiar reverence for the bodies of
their dead, and it would have been a sacrilege
to destroy the mummy even of this heretic.
No thought could be entertained of breaking up
the body upon which the divine touch of king-
ship had fallen : that would have been against
all the sentiments which we know the Egyptians
to have held. The cutting out of the name
of the mummy was sufficient punishment : for
thereby the soul of the king was debarred from
all the benefits of the earthly prayers of his
descendants, and became a nameless outcast,
wandering unrecognised and unpitied through
the vast underworld. It was the name " Akhnaton " which was hated so fiercely ; and one
may perhaps suppose that the priests would have
been willing to substitute the king's earlier

name, Amenophis, upon the mummy had they been pressed to do so. His name and figure as Amenophis IV is not damaged upon the monuments ; but only the representations of him after the adoption of the name Akhnaton have been attacked.

The tomb, polluted by the presence of the heretic, was no longer fit for Tiy to rest in ; and the body of the queen was therefore carried elsewhere, perhaps to the sepulchre of her husband, Amenophis III. The shrine, or outer coffin, in which her mummy had lain was pulled to pieces, and an attempt was made to carry it out of the tomb to its owner's new resting-place, but this arduous task was presently abandoned, and one portion of the shrine was left in the passage, while the rest remained in sections in the burial-chamber. Some of the queen's toilet utensils which had been buried with her were also left, probably by mistake. The body of Akhnaton, his name taken from him, was now the sole occupant of the tomb. The coffin in which it lay rested upon a four-legged bier some two feet or so from the ground, and in a niche in the wall above it stood the four canopic jars. And thus, with a curse, the priests left their great enemy. One of them, before he left the dark chamber of death, ripped off the gold foil from the face of the effigy on the lid of the coffin,

and carried it away, concealed, no doubt, in
his robes.   The entrance of the tomb was blocked
with stones, and sealed with the seal of the
necropolis ; and all traces of its mouth were
hidden by rocks and *débris*.

The priests would not now permit the name of
Akhnaton to pass a man's lips, and by the end
of the reign of Horemheb, the unfortunate boy
was spoken of in official documents as " that
criminal." Not forty years had passed since
Akhnaton's death, yet the priesthood of Amon
was as powerful as it had ever been at any
period of its existence.   There were still living
men who had been old enough at the time of
the Aton power to grasp its doctrines ; and
those same eyes which had looked upon the fair
City of the Horizon might now disturb the
creatures of the desert in the ruined courts where
the grave boy-Pharaoh had presided so lately.
These man joined their voices to that crowd
of priests who, not daring to allow the word
Akhnaton to form itself upon their lips, poured
curses upon the excommunicated and nameless
" criminal." Through starry space their execra-
tions passed, searching out the wretched ghost
of the boy, and banning him, as they supposed,
even in the dim uncertainties of the Lands
of Death.   Over the hills of the west, up the
stairs of the moon, and down into the caverns

under the world, the poor twittering shadow
was hunted and chased by the relentless magic
of the men whom he had tried to reform. There
was no place for his memory upon earth, and in
the under-world the priests denied him a stone
upon which to lay his head. It is not easy
now to realise the full meaning to the Egyptian
of the excommunication of a soul : cut off from
the comforts of human prayers ; hungry, forlorn,
and wholly desolate ; forced at last to whine
upon the outskirts of villages, to snivel upon
the dung-heaps, to rake with shadowy fingers
amidst the refuse of mean streets for fragments
of decayed food with which to allay the pangs
of hunger caused by the absence of funeral-
offerings. To such a pitiful fate the priests of
Amon consigned " the first individual in history " ;
and as an outcast amongst outcasts, a whimpering
shadow in a place of shadows, the men of Thebes
bade us leave the great idealist, doomed, as they
supposed, to the horrors of a life which will
not end, to the misery of a death that brings
no oblivion.

5. THE FINDING OF THE BODY OF AKHNATON

Thus, sheathed in gold, the nameless body
lay, while the fortunes of Egypt rose and fell
and the centuries slid by. A greater teacher
than Akhnaton arose and preached that peace

which the Pharaoh had foreshadowed, and soon all Egypt rang with the new gospel. Then came the religion of Mohammed, and the days of the sword returned. So the years passed, and many a wise man lived his life and disappeared; but the first of the wise men of history lay undiscovered in the heart of the Theban hills.

Now it happened that there was a fissure in the rocks in which the sepulchre was cut, and during the rains of each season a certain amount of moisture managed to penetrate into the chamber. This gradually rotted the legs of the bier upon which Akhnaton's body lay, and at last there came a time when the two legs at the head of the coffin gave way and precipitated the royal body on to the ground. The bandages around the mummy had already fallen almost to powder, and this jerk sent the golden vulture which was resting upon the king's face or breast on to his forehead, where it lay with the tail and claws resting over the left eye-socket of the skull. Presently the two remaining legs of the bier collapsed, and the whole coffin fell to the ground, the lid being partly jerked off, thus revealing the king's head at one end and his feet at the other, from all of which the flesh had rotted away.

In January, 1907, the excavations in the

Valley of the Tombs of the Kings which were being conducted by Mr. Theodore Davis, of Newport, Rhode Island, U.S.A., and supervised by the present writer, on behalf of the Egyptian Government, brought to light the doorway of the tomb, and it was not long before an entrance was effected. A rough stairway led down into the hillside, bringing the excavators to the mouth of the passage, which was entirely blocked by the wall which the priests had built after they had entered the tomb to erase Akhnaton's name. Beyond this wall the passage was found to be nearly choked with the *débris* of the three earlier walls, the first of which had been built after Queen Tiy had been buried here, the second after Akhnaton's agents had entered the tomb to erase the name of Amon, and the third after Akhnaton's body had been laid beside that of his mother. On top of this heap of stones lay the side of the funeral shrine of the queen which the priests had abandoned after attempting to carry it out with her mummy. In the burial-chamber beyond, the remaining portions of this shrine were found. Upon these one saw the figures of Akhnaton and his mother worshipping beneath the rays of the Aton. The inscriptions showed the erasure of the name of Amenophis III, and the substitution in red ink of that king's second name, Nebmaara ; and one observed that at a later date the name and figures of Akhnaton had been hammered out.

At one side lay the coffin of Akhnaton, as it had fallen from the bier. The name of Akhnaton upon the coffin had been erased, but was still readable ; and the gold ribbons from which his name had been cut out still encircled the body, back and front. The golden vulture lay as has been described above, and the necklace still rested on the breast, while the whole decaying body was found to be wrapped in sheets of gold. In a recess above this coffin stood the canopic jars, and in another part of the tomb Queen Tiy's toilet utensils were found, from one of which the name of Amenophis III had been erased.

The coffin was found to be in a state of decay which necessitated the utmost care in its handling ; and it was many months before it was pieced together and placed on exhibition in the Cairo Museum. The inscription engraved on the gold foil beneath the feet[1] was now able to be seen, and this proved to be a short prayer addressed by the king to his God, which one is justified in supposing to have been composed by Akhnaton himself as a kind of epitaph, for it shows signs of having been written upon the coffin later than the main inscription. The

[1] Page 232.

translation, made by Dr. Alan Gardiner, is here published for the first time.

> It reads :—" I breathe the sweet breath which comes forth from Thy mouth. I behold Thy beauty every day. It is my desire that I may hear Thy sweet voice, even the north wind, that my limbs may be rejuvenated with life through love of Thee. Give me Thy hands, holding Thy spirit, that I may receive it and may live by it. Call Thou upon my name unto eternity, and it shall never fail."

There is no need to call the reader's attention to the great pathos of these words addressed by the young king to the god for whom he had lost all. It is evident from them that in the end, when the disasters fell upon him from all sides, his faith remained unshaken, and that, though the death of the body was nigh, he still believed in an endless life of the spirit in which he would be able throughout all eternity to serve his Creator with a love and loyalty which would never fail.

The mummy, which had so fallen to pieces that only the bones remained intact, was sent to the Cairo Museum by the writer, to be examined by Professor Elliot Smith, who reported that they were those of a man of not more than thirty years of age, that is to say the age at which Akhnaton has been shown in these pages to have died. The misshapen skull was pronounced to be that of a man who suffered from epileptic fits and who was probably subject to hallucinations. Curiously enough the peculiarities of the skull are precisely those which Lombroso has stated to be usual in a religious reformer.

6. CONCLUSION

Thus, the body of this the most remarkable figure of early Oriental history was brought to light ; and here we may close this sketch of his life, which has been written for the purpose of introducing the general reader to one of the most interesting characters ever known. In this brief outline it has only been possible to touch upon the main characteristics which the few remaining inscriptions and monuments seem to reveal ; but to the most casual reader it will be apparent that there stands before him a personality of surprising vigour and amazing originality, and one deserving of careful study. In an age of superstition, and in a land where the grossest polytheism reigned absolutely supreme, Akhnaton evolved a monotheistic religion second only to Christianity itself in purity of tone. He was the first human being to understand rightly the meaning of divinity. When the world reverberated with the noise of war, he preached the first known doctrine of peace ; when the glory of martial pomp swelled the hearts of his subjects he deliberately turned his back upon heroics. He was the first man to preach simplicity, honesty, frankness, and sincerity ; and he preached it from a throne. He was the first Pharaoh to be a humanitarian ; the first man in whose heart there was no trace of barbarism. He has given us an example three thousand years ago which might be followed at the present day : an example of what a husband and a father should be, of what an honest man should do, of what a poet should feel, of what a preacher should teach, of what an artist should strive for, of what a scientist should believe, of what a philosopher should think. Like other great teachers he sacrificed all to his principles, and thus his life plainly shows— alas !—the impracticability of his doctrines ; yet there can be no question that his ideals will hold good " till the swan turns black and the crow turns white, till the hills rise up to travel, and the deeps rush into the rivers."

It may be expected that the excavations of the Egypt Exploration Society which are now being conducted on the site of Akhnaton's city will throw a great flood of light upon this amazing epoch of history ; and it is to be hoped that those whose interest in this ancient tragedy— for tragedy it is—has been aroused by these pages will give some sort of financial support, however small, to the work, so that some day the tale may be told with greater accuracy and in fuller detail than in the foregoing pages.

THE END

Printed by
PURNELL AND SONS
PAULTON, ENGLAND

INDEX

THE 18TH DYNASTY MY DATES

① AHMOSES (1825–1800) 25

② AHMENHOTEP I (1803–1780) 23

③ THUTMOSES I (1783–1757) 26

④ THUTMOSES II (1758–1752) 6

⑤ HATSHEPSUT (1763–1730) 33

⑥ THUTMOSES III (1752–1698) 54

⑦ AHMENHOTEP II (1703–1672) 31

⑧ THUTMOSES IV (1673–1655) 18

⑨ AHMENHOTEP III (1657–1617) 40

⑩ AKHNATEN (1620–1599) 21

⑪ SMENKHKARE (1604–1598) 6

OVER

AN—KHE—SENE—AH—MUN

AN—KNUN—SINA—AH—MOON

WIFE OF TUT

FOSTER—MOTHER of MOSES

---

(12) NEFERTITI (1602—1590) 12

(13) TUTANKHEAHMEN (1591—1582) 9

(14) ANKHESENEAHMUN (1583—1582) 1

(15) AYE (1582—1578) 4

(16) HOREMHEB (1578—1543) 35

THE DAUGHTERS OF AKHENATEN

(1) MERITATEN

(2) MEKETATEN

(3) ANKHESENEAHMUN

(4) NEFERNEFRURE

(5) NEFERFRUATEN?

(6) SETEP SITRA?

(7) NEFRURE?

OTHER COOPER SQUARE PRESS TITLES OF INTEREST

HANNIBAL
G. P. Baker
366 pp., 3 b/w illustrations, 5 maps
0-8154-1005-0
$16.95

HISTORY OF THE CONQUEST OF MEXICO &
HISTORY OF THE CONQUEST OF PERU
William H. Prescott
1330 pp., 2 maps
0-8154-1004-2
$29.95

AGINCOURT
Christopher Hibbert
176 pp., 33 b/w illustrations, 3 maps
0-8154-1053-0
$16.95

THE DREAM AND THE TOMB
A History of the Crusades
Robert Payne
456 pp., 37 b/w illustrations, 11 maps
0-8154-1086-7
$19.95

AUGUSTUS
The Golden Age of Rome
G. P. Baker
376 pp., 17 b/w illustrations, 8 maps
0-8154-1089-1
$18.95